Language
Is Everything

How Words Can Change Your Life

ANNA JIANG, PHD

Supported by Beijing Normal University
(Grant number: 105567GK)

Cover design by **Wenqi Kang.**

Published by **Sai Blackbyrn.**

ISBN: 978-1-8382522-0-5

Anna Jiang was born and grew up in China. She is a linguist, simultaneous interpreter and lecturer at Beijing Normal University. She holds a PhD in language education from UCL (University College London) Institute of Education. For more than a decade, Anna has been committed to teaching and researching education and language from a cross-disciplinary perspective. She is particularly interested in the ways that language plays a role in how we live and learn. After a traumatic life event forced Anna to reconsider her path, both spiritually and professionally, she moved onto a new stage of her career. She's now an educator and speaker, but more importantly, she's a certified NeuroCoach who uses her own experience along with the wisdom of neuroscience to help people become the person they are truly happy with and manifest the life they desire. She advocates brain-based experiential learning in the educational field.

You can contact her at: *annayqjiang@qq.com.*

This book is dedicated to everyone who had the courage to say goodbye to their old lives and start a new chapter. But, most especially, this book is for Marco.

CONTENTS

Preface

*"The job of the linguist, like that of the biologist, is not to tell us how
nature should behave, or what its creations should look like, but to describe
those creations in all their messy glory and try to figure out what they can
teach us about life, the world, and, especially in the case of linguistics, the
workings of the human mind."*

Arika Okrent[1]

I'm a linguist and an interpreter. I investigate how we make meaning from
words, how words trigger our feelings, and how language shapes our reality.
Two decades of working with language closely has developed my sensitivity
to language, particularly how it changes across cultures and contexts.
Language influences the way we experience ourselves in the world; It defines
who we are and how we think and feel.

I've also learned that language is malleable. You can look up the meaning of
a single word in a dictionary, but it is never fixed in stone. The meanings of
words evolve alongside the culture that speaks them. Each person's experience
of language also evolves with time, practice, and experience. And just as
language is susceptible to change, so are we.

I'm also an educator. I've been teaching in a Chinese university for more than
ten years. I'm committed to motivating students to change their lives for the
better. With a focus on the role that language plays in learning, my mission
is to bring about transformation through the power of language and learning.

My inquiry into the relationship between language and the brain has led me
to take up an interest in neuroscience. In particular, I'm fascinated by how
language plays a role in shaping our thoughts and feelings and how cognition
and emotion are connected through language. With over a decade of

experience of motivating students in the classroom, I now apply all that I've learned in my work as a coach. I'm trained in NeuroCoaching. Unlike other forms of personal development and business coaching—which are primarily anchored in traditional, psychological, cognitive, or metaphysical theories—NeuroCoaching involves new forms of mindful communication and intuitive problem-solving that have emerged from the collaborative brain-scan research of Andrew Newberg (Jefferson University), Mark Waldman, and Chris Manning (both from Loyola Marymount University).

These brain-based, evidence-based, and mindfulness-based strategies have been shown to alter specific brain networks in ways that enhance one's intuitive ability to calmly find creative solutions to virtually any obstacle or problem: in the workplace and at home; in personal relationships and social situations; and for reducing stress, anxiety, and emotional trauma. It is an experiential process using a unique form of mutual dialog that gives you new tools that you can easily integrate into your daily life.

This book is a result of my years of observation and investigation into language as a linguist, interpreter, and educator and how I apply that knowledge to my coaching. It's about all the ways that language affects our daily lives. But it's unlike other books on linguistics. Here's why: I focus on the power of language to affect our minds, shape our realities, and influence the experiences of our emotions. When we transform the story we tell ourselves, we can reinvent ourselves and create the life we want. At its core, this is a self-help book.

So, what is in it for you? Well, it helps you:

- Develop greater sensitivity to language and improve your skills of empathy, especially when communicating with people from different cultures and backgrounds.
- Gain insight into how the story you tell yourself shapes your experience and learn how to write a new story that empowers and inspires you.

- Identity your values and live by them, so you can live a life full of meaning and purpose.
- Set goals for your life that connect with your highest values and develop a concrete plan for achieving them.
- Get in touch with your feelings, manage difficult emotions, and find peace and happiness.
- Develop insight into the power of language and use that to become the best version of yourself possible.

With its focus on language and its emphasis on a cross-cultural perspective, this book is also unlike any other self-help book. It provides in-depth and specialized research that unpacks the beauty and mechanics of language, our brains, and our lives. It will change the way you think about yourself.

In many ways, this book echoes some of the teachings present across ancient wisdom traditions, which is where the contemporary practice of mindfulness originates. One of the most popular books on Buddhism, which introduced many Americans to the tradition, is *The Way of Zen* by Alan Watts. In it, Watts quotes the 9th century Zen Master Seigen Ishin, which I understand as a profound meditation of the relationship of language and the mind. He says,

> "Before I had studied Zen for 30 years, I saw mountains as mountains, and waters as waters. When I arrived at a more intimate knowledge, I came to the point where I saw that mountains are not mountains, and waters are not waters. But now that I have got its very substance I am at rest. For it's just that I see mountains once again as mountains, and waters once again as waters."[2]

It's my hope that this book helps you arrive, like Seigen Ishin, at a "more intimate knowledge" of your life. It's designed to open a window, so you can come to see your life from an entirely new perspective—with an open mind. By practicing the exercises in this book, like Seigen Ishin, you can learn to see the "substance" of anything—a mountain, yourself, or the world you live in—by first seeing it as something other than what you think it is. When you consistently practice mindful awareness of words, language, and your story, it's inevitable that you'll gain a fresh understanding of yourself, the world, and the relationship between the two. I hope this book helps facilitate that process.

I also hope that this book encourages you to reconsider what language is to you and to see how it is integrated in your life. A fresh, in-depth understanding of language will shift how you experience your life. Learning a second language can also offer you a new frame of reference, a new way of representing the world. But you don't have to learn a second language to experience the power of language. If you are reading this book right now, you've already acquired at least one language. You, like everyone, are immersed in language. Once you understand its power, you'll develop insights into how to harness that power to change your life and manifest the life you desire.

Here's how the structure of the book looks like:

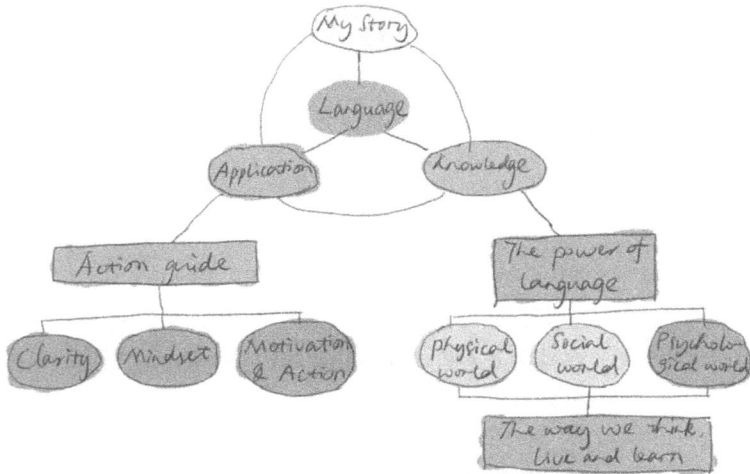

Figure 1

Part one of this book tells my own story – my journey of discovering and experiencing the power of language. Part two informs you the knowledge for change – the lesser-known secret about language that introduces you to a new world and a new life. Part three walks you through the application of that knowledge. It offers practical action guides in chapters seven, eight, and nine to help you reset your mindset, identify your values, and consciously live by them so that you are motivated and take action to manifest the life you desire. The steps I encourage you to take are easy to follow. They've proven effective in the work I've done with friends, students, and clients. But taking action is key if you want to change your life and manifest the life you desire. Follow the steps closely. But, be aware that you might not see results overnight. Just like the conditioning of a muscle, the training of your mind takes time.

Neurotips and brain-based strategies throughout this book have been designed to help you overcome emotional distress, nurture a healthy brain, and boost your mental energy. They'll help you tap into your intuition, creativity, and deepest potential. These tips and strategies are grounded in contemporary research into the brain, and they are backed up with evidence from brain-imaging. Whenever possible, I've referenced the sources of this research, which have been published in peer-reviewed journals. Some of this research lies at the intersection of linguistics, applied linguistics, philosophy, sociology, psychology, and neuroscience. When it comes to language, the boundaries between these disciplines become blurred. I believe language has the potential to connect these disciplines.

If you are a graduate student or teacher embarking on research in linguistics, you are welcome to read this book. It offers cross-disciplinary perspectives you likely won't come across in any other book on linguistics. If you are not interested in language (though I think it's impossible for anyone to have *no* interest in language since we live so deeply within it), but you are looking for ways to change your life and manifest the life you desire, there's no doubt you will benefit from the exercises and neurotips I mention.

At heart, this book is for anyone who wants to discover themselves through the power of language. It's for anyone who wants to access their innate power to achieve whatever goal they desire. By harnessing the power of language, I ascended and transcended from the darkest days of my life. And then, I reinvented my own life. I hope this book can help you do the same.

Part 1

How Did Words Change My Life?

The two-decade experience of learning a second language and working with it sensitized me toward the hidden power of language. My story of rising above from the darkest days of my life provided me with enlightened views and knowledge about how language transforms lives. In this first part, I will take you through my journey of discovering and experiencing the power of language.

Chapter 1: Experiencing the Power of Language

"It is said that life and death are under the power of language."

Helene Cixous[3]

"Language is power, in ways more literal than most people think. When we speak, we exercise the power of language to transform reality. Why don't more of us realize the connection between language and power?"

Julia Penelope[4]

"Thought is the blossom; language the bud; action the fruit behind it."

Ralph Waldo Emerson[5]

"Words are, of course, the most powerful drug used by mankind."

Rudyard Kipling[6]

There was a spring in my life that I will never forget. That was the spring that I barely slept. Lying awake beside my one-year-old son, a little angel drifting off in the darkness, I struggled to hold back the tears. My husband had stopped communicating months ago. I couldn't bear the thought of our son growing up without a father. How was I going to manage it all? Working at the university and struggling to finish my PhD, I felt like I was living in a tunnel with no light in sight. Vulnerable and full of fear, I began falling into a depression.

Things, however, took big turns very shortly. In that summer, my husband and I divorced. Before Christmas, I got an email from the university confirming the award of my PhD. Today, I'm an author, a university lecturer and a Neurocoach. I am independent, happy and fulfilled.

How did I end up in this happy place? How did I get from that sleepless spring to where I am now—happy, content, and in control? I believe anyone can rise out of a seemingly impossible situation. Change is not as miraculous as you may think. Often, all it takes is a shift of mindset and a clear set of steps to set you in the right direction. Let me tell you how I did it.

Dirty laundry

My husband was a good, traditional Chinese man. He worked as a banker. When I first met him, I adored our conversations. He seemed to know everything under the sun. I appreciated the different perspectives he offered me. But after I gave birth to our son, things started to change quickly. Eventually, we reached a state where communication felt impossible, but I didn't know how we ended up there. All I know is that our conversations went something like this:

Me: "I'm exhausted. I need to get up three, four or five times a night to comfort our baby."

Him: "Are you suggesting that I'm the one who is leading an easy life?"

I did not know what to say. I felt even more depressed.

Me: "I need to finish my PhD. My career depends on it! But with the baby, I hardly have any time to write."

Him: "I told you that you ought to have finished it before you had the baby!"

I was lost for words. I didn't know whether to blame him or myself.

Me: "I think my mom gets tired helping us out. Can you be nice to her? Please don't ignore her when she comes over."

Him: "I'm already nice to her. Don't focus on what I say or not say, look what I do."

Me: "What did you do?"

Him: "Can't you see what I do?"

……

I began to wonder whether I truly knew the man I had married. It seemed like he didn't know me either. To him, our communication breakdown was no big deal. He said he was happy in our marriage. For me, I just became a new mom, struggling to learn a new grammar whose rules are made up by my baby. My days had become a long sentence in the present continuous, which did not speak to the future. I felt exhausted; I was drowning. I needed care and love desperately. But I didn't feel needed or cared about—let alone loved. My self-esteem evaporated into a haze of loneliness, helplessness, and desperation. Nearly at the point of breaking down, my suffering eluded him. He insisted all was well. At last, I suggested that we go to a therapist—it was my last resort. He said therapists don't solve problems. Besides, to him, we had no problems to solve.

Therapy had been my final hope for my marriage. My husband's denial drove us further apart. I began to see how our core values differed. When we first met, we seemed to understand each other. But we expected different things of marriage. We lived in separate worlds and spoke two different languages. What was obvious to me was that there was no hope of translating between the two. He was a stranger from a strange land. Ironically, language and cross-cultural communication were my academic expertise. I had studied both for more than two decades. With people from vastly different cultural backgrounds, I spoke effortlessly. But with the person I was most intimate with, communication felt impossible. In my marriage, my skills of communication failed to deliver.

It was clear that divorce was the only way out, but the decision did not come easily to me. I had to consider the consequences on my little son. Like most new mothers, I wanted the best for my baby. In the end, I had to choose the lesser of two evils.

When I said to him, "I want a divorce," his reply shocked me.

"Don't you dare to threaten me!" My husband said.

He thought I was crazy to throw away the "good" life. But his words made it more painfully obvious that I had never known who he was. I wanted desperately to get out of a marriage that was suffocating me. He didn't want to end the marriage, but he didn't want to work through its problems either. To him, our marriage wasn't broken—so why fix it? Why end it?

Some couples come together because they want to get to know each other. Once they grow familiar, the intrigue vanishes, and the couple drifts apart. My husband and I came together because we thought we knew each other. We drifted apart when it was clear we didn't.

Phoenix rising

So, there I was: a supposedly crazy woman who had left her husband, a soon-to-be divorced woman who had exchanged the good life for the lonely life of a single mother. My husband wasn't responding to my messages. I was scared to hell. I wasn't afraid because of what I imagined he might do to me. I was frightened because of what I imagined his absence might do to our son.

When I saw other fathers on the street take their child's hand, there would be a lump in my throat. I sometimes got emotional. Had my husband disappeared forever? Would I be both mother and father to our son? I had to provide for him, but I didn't know how I would emerge from the shadows of a failed marriage. How would I finish my PhD? When would I be happy? When would I be strong? I wanted to raise a happy, strong kid. But neither strength nor happiness flourish in the absence of hope. And I was rapidly losing hope.

My fears and uncertainties kept me up at night. Every time I looked at my son, I felt a mix of regret and guilt. After a good cry, my brain seemed to work again. It was only after shedding an ocean of tears that I had an epiphany. For my boy to grow up in an environment filled with happiness and love, I had to be filled with happiness and love. Since I was his mother, I had to create the best conditions for him to grow up in. I had to be strong.

I had to protect him from harm. There was no room for negotiation. "To be or not to be," was not a question I could afford to ask myself. I had to be there for my child. I had to take action then and there.

So, I changed the story I was telling myself. Remarkably, my situation transformed. I began to see the beauty in having only one option. Achieving clarity about what I had to do and who I had to become was the best thing that could have happened to me. It helped me strip away the inessentials and focus on what mattered most. It empowered me. It made me unstoppable. I may have still harbored fears, but I wore new armor against them. As Franklin D. Roosevelt said at the height of the Great Depression, "The only thing we have to fear … is fear itself."

Amidst my own great depression, I was determined to take Roosevelt's words to heart. I had to save myself from drowning in my own fears. I focused on the things I had to do. My years of experience as a teacher and as a home-schooled student had taught me that the best way to lead was by example. I had to be a good example to my son. I needed to be the best me possible. I knew that it would be riskier to remain tight in bud than to blossom into a full flower. It was my time to bloom, to fulfill my potential, and to live life to the fullest.

Before my marriage, I had pursued many passions. I have an eye for art and for beauty. I had practiced calligraphy for more than a decade. I am passionate about language and the study of language and communication. The power of education to motivate people, to transform their minds and hearts, has always amazed me.

But when I was struggling in my marriage, I stopped pursuing my interests passionately. I lost my drive. When the marriage ended, I had to rediscover who I was and achieve clarity about what I had to do. I knew I needed to finish my PhD. It wasn't just that I needed the degree to move on in my career. I was researching the nature of learning and teaching; my project was an inquiry into human thinking. The topic was valuable, and I was passionate about it. I had already collected the data. I just need to finish the data analysis and write the thesis.

In many ways, pursuing a PhD is like undertaking any big project. It's easy to get started, but it's painfully difficult to complete. You inevitably feel stuck. At times, it eats you up. It consumes you. I procrastinated. My reading of the literature never seemed sufficient. The writing never seemed good enough. I doubted whether I was suited to do research in the first place.

But when I began telling myself that I had to finish it no matter what, I was unstoppable. I stopped feeling afraid of the challenges and mired in the difficulties. I did whatever it took. I set myself a deadline, broke the work into manageable chunks, and hit my daily writing targets.

Once I had clarity about what I had to do, the only problem I faced was time. For a single mom with a one-year-old toddler, time is the most precious thing. But if you have to do something, you make time for it. So, I went to bed at ten, got up at four in the morning and wrote until nine a.m. Whenever I had free time in between teaching and attending my baby, I wrote. Writing became my daily habit. Two months on, I finished a draft of my thesis. Then, I heard from my ex-husband, when he sent me our divorce papers.

The word "divorce" no longer disturbed the peace in my heart. I had let go of feeling like a victim of a failed marriage. I had given up playing a supporting role in my own life. I had taken center stage. I was the leading lady. Failing in my marriage didn't mean failing in my life. Just because one relationship didn't work, it doesn't mean my relationships with others would fail. Besides, I had developed an understanding about what worked in a marriage and what didn't. I saw how I could benefit from my experience.

In the darkest days of living in the shadow of a broken marriage, it would have been all too easy to have fallen into a trap of negative thinking. The popular discourse in China of the divorced woman would paint me as a failed wife, a woman not worthy of love, a mother who let her son grow up without a father only for him to have problems in adulthood. Conventional thinking says that only pain comes in the wake of a broken home. But I didn't have to live my life according to that thinking. I may have let go of my marriage, but in giving up on one path, another unfolded. Having less can offer more. With fewer marital problems to worry about, it was easier to direct my attention to what mattered most.

Books on parenting often teach single moms to make up for a missing father. Our culture is quick to see the absence of a father as undesirable and a single mother as deserving of pity. But two parents do not by default parent better than one. If a couple is struggling, the conflicts and underlying tension often negatively affect the well-being of their child, too. It is hard to find a family where no harm has been done. Even the most protected family environments can leave children feeling vulnerable. If kids are not exposed to the tests and challenges of life, they may be ill-prepared for adulthood. If guided appropriately, they can come to understand loss. They can develop strength of character and resilience for whatever might come. Children who have experienced loss early in life learn to cherish what they have. They learn to appreciate the present.

So, I embraced an entirely new narrative. The old one went something like this: "How are you going to live a happy life without a husband?" and "How is your child going to grow up properly without a father?" Whereas, the new narrative empowered me. It went like this: "Nothing will diminish my strength and my happiness" and "I will be a happy and strong mom and will raise a happy and strong kid."

The new story began to work its magic.

I felt strong, and I felt happy.

I was, most definitely, unstoppable.

Discovering the power of language

Once I changed the narrative and the words I spoke to myself, life turned around for me. I no longer lived under the shadow of anyone or anything. I no longer saw my failed marriage as a loss, but it was a clear win. I felt less like a victim and more like a hero. I was in charge of my own narrative and at the helm of my own life, just like any leading lady. With a new narrative, I had taken a new lease on life, one that came with a new mindset and a new, healthy brain. From the depth of depression, desperation, and divorce, I developed into a happy single mom—a doctor—who had new hopes for the future.

Language, I realized, had the power to transform any situation. We are all linguistic beings. We live in language in the same way that fish live in water. The words other people use to describe us can make a significant impact on us, especially the negative words, the cruel ones. If someone you love tells you that you have failed as a partner, you rarely forget it. If your mother tells you that you are always wrong, you carry those words with you for years. Just as it is easy to remember the insults, it can be difficult to remember the praise. Your partners or parents may have said many kind things to you. But we tend to forget those kind words. It's perfectly normal. Our evolutionary brain has learned to stay alert when encountering anything that threatens our survival.[7] Negative words linger for that reason.

But far more powerful than the words people tell you are the words you tell yourself. Far more influential than the stories others narrate to you are the stories you narrate to yourself. You tell stories to explain and interpret what happens to you. Your stories are not objective truths. They arise from subjective interpretations. They embody your sense of self; they negotiate your identity. A product of how your mind works, stories offer an embellished version of reality, one that appeals to the ways you view yourself and the world. How you speak to yourself can either lift you up or pull you down. If you take charge and change the story, you can change the way you see the world. And if you can change the way you see the world, you can change how you experience your life.

Making best use of the power of words

Discovering the transformative power of language was an immense delight. I knew that I could not afford to ignore it, but only make the best use of it every single day. I started to write down one or two affirmative sentences every morning, to mark a fresh beginning. They keep me motivated for a whole day to achieve my daily goals. For example, the affirmations I wrote today are, "Anna has a lot to offer to the world. She's a great writer who makes a big difference." These words anchor my mind in a positive, uplifting state where I can harness my best potential to write and produce great work.

I also found that writing down your life goals or who you want to become and putting it on the wall or anywhere you can see easily has the same effect. It works even better if you can put a picture along with the words—one depicting the situation when you have achieved your life goal or have become who you want to be. Images help the brain visualize easily. They help reset your brain with a positive mindset, helping you stay motivated to achieve your life goal.

The affirmations you practice daily can be in any form you like, as long as it appeals to you. Let your creative mind decide which works best for you. You can write one or two sentences, you can draw a picture, or you can also create a piece of artwork. For me, I especially like poems. As the American poet and essayist Adrienne Rich said, "Poetry is above all a concentration of the power of language, which is the power of our ultimate relationship to everything in the universe."[8] I find that the process of writing poetry itself is stimulating and empowering. It gives me inspiration and power every time I read it as well!

The following poem is one I wrote for myself when I was struggling with the feeling of "being not good enough" and scared of what others might talk about me. In writing it, I found the courage to be just who I am, by appreciating my uniqueness. I hope by reading it, you discover the unique beauty and power hidden in you as well!

I'm a little little peacock
in a big big world
I'm known for my iridescent tail
When I spread the covert out
It forms a flashy train

But I had so much fear
That I was not good enough
not agile when I was with cats
not fierce with dogs
And not powerful with tigers

I simply forgot to look back at my tail and see its colors
But when I do remember
I keep telling myself that I'm a pretty pretty peacock
So much that the saying starts to act back upon me

I'm a pretty pretty peacock
In a big big world
I'm not afraid to be seen
I'm not afraid to be talked about
It's not a big deal that I'm not agile like a cat,
fierce like a dog
or powerful like a tiger
These qualities do not mean much for a peacock
It's not a big deal that
cats, dogs, and tigers can not appreciate my beauty
It's not a big deal that
They don't like me
I don't need it as a pretty pretty peacock

But I'm grateful for them, all the same
They teach me to understand what I'm made of

They teach me to love myself

In this big big world
We are all different
Yet we all seek nourishment, belonging and fulfillment
We all desire to love and to be loved
We are more similar than different
And we all live in this same world

Sometimes I can see the cat, the dog or the tiger in me myself
Sometimes I can see the peacock in a cat, dog or tiger
Hence familiarity in the other
And otherness in the self
We can agree to disagree
And find harmony in diversity
What a beautiful world we live in

In this big big world
I'm a peacock from outside
But deep inside I am just ME
And I can be anything I choose to be
I'm beautiful for who I am
My beauty comes from within
The peace and power in my mind and heart
Nobody can be ME better than myself

In Summary

Dear reader, I shared with you, in this chapter, how I rose to a happy place from the lowest point in my life. The following diagram (*Figure 2*) demonstrates what triggered the changes and how language played a role in the process. For me, the transformation came when I took charge and changed the story I told myself. Language, indeed, had the power to transform any situation. By making the best use of the power of words, you can change the story you tell yourself and change your life, just like what I did. To do this, you can start practicing affirmations daily. It will anchor your mind in a positive, uplifting state where you can harness your potential to achieve whatever you want for your life.

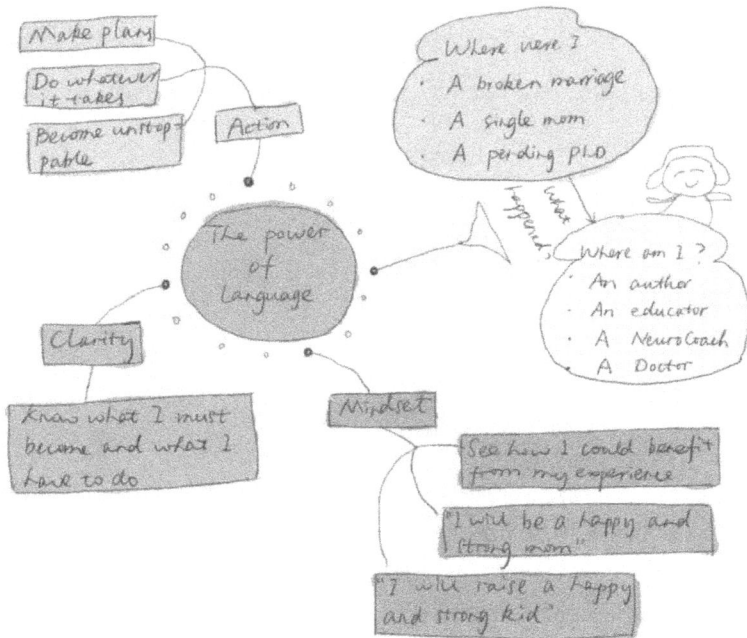

Figure 2

Chapter 2: Understanding the Power of Language through the Lens of a Second Language

"One language sets you in a corridor for life. Two languages open every door along the way."

Frank Smith[9]

"You can never understand one language until you understand at least two."

Geoffrey Willans[10]

"He who knows no foreign language knows nothing of his own."

Johann Wolfgang Von Goethe[11]

I t took, for me, going through a divorce to discover how transformative language can be. However, I have always had a distinct feeling that language is so much more than a tool for communication. It shapes the way we perceive ourselves and the world. It entwines with our act of living through every word we hang on to and every story we tell. It transforms lives in a way that is not being aware of for those whose lives have been changed. My feeling about the power of language comes from my two-decade experience of learning a second language—English—and working with it closely.

Now, let me ask you: Have you tried learning another language? Perhaps you studied French from textbooks and teachers in school. Or you picked up a little Italian when you were singing along to opera in your kitchen. Or maybe on a long flight to Zurich, you spent a few hours studying pocket-sized phrase books—one in German and the other in French—to help you speak the bilingual Swiss.

Even if you don't speak a second language fluently, no doubt you've picked up a few foreign phrases. You may know next to no Yiddish, but you know that a guy with *chutzpah* has a lot of confidence. You may not understand Italian, but you've likely walked into a Starbucks and ordered a *caffè latte.* You may have little grasp of French, but when you've felt you've experienced something twice, you may have called it *déjà-vu.*

When I meet people who speak a second language, I often ask: *How has that language changed you?* Some people say that learning a new language has kept them from getting lost. Learning Spanish before heading to Argentina means you can ask for directions in Buenos Aires in the local language if you've lost your way in the Plaza del Mayo. Language has a practical purpose.

Others say that despite the awkward part at the beginning, learning a language makes them feel good. But when I ask those same people to dig a little deeper—*Why does learning a language make you feel good?*—nearly everyone falls silent.

Perhaps I need to start by asking a different question. *How has your college education changed you?* might be a better way to start the conversation. People appreciate that college changes who they are. Like learning a new language, people tend to think of college as a practical decision. The career-oriented amongst us might say that a college education has heightened their skillset, job prospects, and social status. But often it doesn't end there. Most people agree that college can shape their lives in ways that aren't necessarily practical. A recent graduate might reflect on how he met his fiancé in college, which led him to do impractical things, like elope before graduation. Another might say that college was where he first read Kierkegaard, which led him to switch majors from pre-med to philosophy.

But what if you're well past graduation and have forgotten all that you learned in college? You may have left behind the books you read, but that doesn't mean those books haven't continued to influence you. "Education," said Albert Einstein, "is what remains when one has forgotten everything he learned in school."[12] Those early lessons, long forgotten, continue to make an impact on who you are, what you do, and how you approach each day— often without you even noticing.

Learning anything—whether molecular biology, British history, or Dutch grammar—slowly and covertly changes you. Your mother tongue may shape how you see, think, and behave. But speaking an additional language gives you access to another way of representing the world. As the Italian filmmaker Federico Fellini said, "A different language is a different vision of life."[13]

If you were raised in Japan, you most likely rely on Japanese to make sense of your experience. If English is your mother tongue, you depend on English words and phrases to reflect on your place in the world. But if you're bilingual, you have two languages to represent and process the world. You have two frames of reference, two cultures. It may take years of studying a new language to fully appreciate its impact on you. But if you practice a second language long enough, it can transform how you see the world—and yourself.

For two decades, I've been learning English. I've immersed myself in its vocabulary, grammar and culture. I've also been studying the influence that the English language has on my mind. To me, learning English not only means gaining a practical tool that offers a little personal satisfaction on the side. Of course, knowing English helps me get from Charing Cross to Piccadilly Circus when I visit London, England. But the functionality of language is not what intrigues me. Just as a zoologist finds wonder in the evolution of bats or a professor of poetry dedicates years to unveiling hidden gems in a collection of sonnets, I explore language. I am mesmerized by all its forms, beauty, and peculiarities.

In the more than two decades that I've been learning English, I've learned that the real rewards of learning a language rarely come right away. I've only just begun to see how language shapes not only culture but a sense of self. Grasping that connection has helped me to unlock secrets of how I might live a more engaged, pleasurable, and meaningful life.

But secrets are only half as fun when you keep them to yourself.

Gaining a deeper understanding of language can transform your life, too.

When your perception of language changes, you'll begin to see how intimately the words you use shape how you experience each moment. A more profound understanding of language can transform how you experience reality. That knowledge can give you the power to shape the direction of your life.

Rebel language

Before I share my discoveries of language, let me tell you how I got here. Like most kids who grew up in China in the 1980s and '90s, I began studying English in junior high school. I learned quickly that Chinese and English are remarkably different languages. Chinese uses an ideographical writing system, one based on meaning rather than sound. English uses an alphabetic writing system, one based on sound rather than meaning. In Chinese, characters represent ideas. In English, letters or groups of letters represent distinct sounds, called phonemes, which when strung together represent words and ideas.

Take the expression, "It's nice to meet you." Now, say it aloud. Notice how the discrete sounds, or phonemes, flow together. Notice how the 't' sound at the end of 'meet' links with the 'y' sound at the beginning of 'you.' If English is your native tongue, you join those sounds in speech without thinking about it. But for someone whose native tongue is Chinese, the flow between English sounds, especially at the end and beginnings of words, comes only with careful practice.

Unlike my friends in junior high, when I first began to learn English, I didn't struggle. With only a little practice, I could easily pronounce English phrases. As if by instinct, I linked the "t" sound at the end "meet" with the "y" sound at the beginning of "you" when I said, "It's nice to meet you." That surprised my teacher, who told my parents that I had a knack for it. For most kids in China, reciting the spelling and pronunciation of words feels like a chore. For me, it was a piece of cake. Grammar, which most kids meet with dread, never fazed me. English teachers loved me. I breezed right through all the lessons. I felt confident, enthusiastic, and on top of the world.

But when I entered senior high school, all that changed. The unfamiliarity of a new school challenged my sense of belonging. A year before, I had been on cloud nine; In senior high school, I fell off of it. My self-confidence plummeted. My grades suffered. Speaking English still came effortlessly to me, but my English teacher—who was at the time our class teacher—saw me as a troubled teenager. Instead of using my finesse with words to win her over, I used them as a weapon, often in defense. I began to take solace in the things that made me different. When classmates struggled to form English sentences, I polished off perfectly-pronounced paragraphs. When I spoke English, I imagined I was rising above the crowd and floating above all my worries.

Through the English language, I found the courage to speak my mind. The sad, shy and uneasy Chinese teenager disappeared the moment I started speaking my new language. I argued confidently with my English teacher. When I spoke English, I felt like I was dancing. Another person—hidden inside me—leaped out. I didn't recognize that person. Nor did my parents. She was enthusiastic and self-assured. From that moment on, I knew that language had real power. That power had been concealed within me all along. Let me also tell you that it's possible in your case, too. The power is within you.

Two languages, two selves

Naturally, I went on to major in English in college. Higher education gave me endless opportunities to read books, write papers, and carry on conversations in my beloved second language. I kept an English journal and wrote in it daily. At one corner of campus, a designated "English corner," students spoke only English. I went there regularly, feeling right at home. Not only did I feel in my element, the sounds of English excited and intrigued me. Not only was I learning a new language, I was learning a new perspective on life.

Initiation into a new culture, however, is not always that easy. The English writer G.K. Chesterton describes the gaps in understanding between two cultures in his 1922 book *What I Saw in America*. Chesterton begins one chapter with an English saying that depicts the awkwardness of learning a new language. "A foreigner," he writes, "is a man who laughs at everything except jokes."[14] To laugh at a joke, you first need to have intimate knowledge of the culture. If you don't, you may find everything in the new culture funny—except the jokes! You also learn to accept that people in another culture will find you funny and not understand your jokes. I have experienced this myself.

When I first visited England, even though I spoke English, I found it tricky to make sense of all the puns and wordplay people used. I had no problem understanding lectures given by professors, but I had difficulty understanding the small talk of shopkeepers, waiters, and bartenders, especially those with a thick British accent. I didn't get the jokes. If you've been to England, you know that small talk and cheeky humor are a big part of British culture. So, you can imagine how much of an outsider I felt like when small talk and jokes went right over my head! No doubt, some British people might have found my accent funny and difficult to understand, just as I had a hard time understanding theirs.

But in my experience, the culture shock turned quickly into comradery with an open mind. After spending enough time in England, I got used to the small talk. The accent no longer confused me. I picked up on the cheeky humor and enjoyed the local slang. I understood how to chit chat with the shopkeeper and the bartender. I began to appreciate the wit and ways of the Brits. Appreciating the quirks of a foreign culture helped me find humor in my own, too. I eventually found that in English, I could express myself in ways I couldn't in Chinese.

Living between two cultures and speaking two languages taught me that, despite superficial differences, we all share common concerns and core emotions. Similar drives motivate us as a species. We all seek nourishment, belonging, and fulfillment. The culture you grow up in inevitably shapes the ways you behave. But the motivation for the behavior comes from neurological tendencies that we all share.

To explain the pleasure I felt learning English, it helps to look at what might have been happening in my brain. The neural experience of motivation is common across our species. The research of the Estonian neuroscientist and psychobiologist Jaak Panksepp has contributed significantly to my understanding. His theories have shaped many of the ideas of this book. Panksepp coined the term "SEEKING" to describe the positive feelings behind motivation. Those feelings of "I can do this" or "I want to do this" are wired in us. There is a common neural nature for humans and other mammals. When SEEKING is triggered by stimuli, it releases dopamine, which motivates our brain to go after a particular goal or desire.[15] That isn't to say that our cultural differences are trivial. It's important to embrace them.

For example, if you look at the ways that people around the world greet each other, you'll notice both the cultural differences and the core human needs and tendencies underpinning social interactions. When the English meet each other, they say: "How are you?" or "How are you doing?" In China, we say "Hello" to people we first meet and "Have you eaten?" to friends or acquaintances. If you're not from East Asia, that greeting may sound strange to you.

But consider how essential and universal the daily routine of eating is. In China, most people eat three times a day. When two people meet, it's either before or after a meal. Culturally, China values rituals and ceremony. So, asking a friend about one of the most fundamental daily rituals makes sense in its cultural context. Eating is woven into the social fabric of everyday life. Businessmen strike deals at dinner tables. Friends express thanks by inviting each other over for a meal. Families and relatives update each other on their lives at the dinner table.

When you meet a friend on the street and begin the conversation with "Have you eaten?" you may find out that, like you, she hasn't. If you're both hungry, you may end up going to a restaurant together. Asking if a friend has eaten demonstrates care and concern for that friend's well-being, which acts as a type of glue to social relations.

Just as the Chinese custom to ask "Have you eaten?" puzzles outsiders, the British custom to talk about the weather baffles more than a few visitors to the United Kingdom. British weather is famously unpredictable. It makes sense culturally to talk about it now and again. But there's more behind the British obsession with talking about the weather than mere forecast fluctuation. In her book *Watching the English,* the social anthropologist Kate Fox suggests that "weather talk" helps Brits overcome their social inhibitions. Asking someone on the tube in London, "cold, innit?" acts as an ice-breaker. How that person answers—whether with a grumble or smile—tells you what mood she's in and if she's up for a chat.[16]

When I was studying at a UK university, it surprised me when my teachers smiled and said "Hello" to students who arrived late to class. Traditional Chinese teachers reproach latecomers. They might give the student an intimidating look or say something like, "You're ten minutes late!" or "Don't be late next time!" While it hasn't happened to me, I imagine it would be embarrassing. "Hello" is far more inviting. It sounds friendlier. It's not that Chinese teachers are unfriendly, but the way they greet latecomers reflects China's tradition of strict discipline. It demonstrates the high expectations Chinese teachers hold for their students.

In England, at the university level, respect, and equality between teachers and students is the norm rather than the exception. I think it's important for students to have a sense of discipline, but I also appreciate how English teachers welcome their students. When I was in that atmosphere, it gave me the courage to speak my mind. With a greater sense of equality, I found it easier to challenge the teacher. When I spoke my mind, I felt more engaged and I learned more. Now, as I teach, I incorporate both high expectations and respect and equality between my students and myself. In doing that, I manage to create a safe learning environment where students are not afraid to make a mistake while presented with challenging tasks and willing to take the risk of offering different perspectives.

Becoming aware of cultural differences led me to understand myself better. I was able to see why, coming from China, I acted in culturally-specific ways. I imagine to my British friends, I may have come across as rather formal. I recognized for the first time that I had taken my cultural idiosyncrasies for granted.

It is all too easy to go to a foreign country and focus on the differences. If you go to Finland, you may notice the Finnish tendency toward discretion and modesty. If you hop on a plane to Italy, you might notice people using a lot of hand gestures to tell a story. But can you look at your own culture from the advantage point of an outsider? Perhaps you already have. If you're Dutch, you may appreciate how growing up in the Netherlands has influenced your preference for stating your opinions frankly. But when you travel to England, can you appreciate the ways that Brits—having grown up in a culture that encourages a stiff upper lip—express their feelings indirectly, so much so that they'd rather talk about the weather?

To speak a foreign language is to engage in the process of what the late Cambridge Professor Barry Jones describes as "exploring otherness."[17] When I lived in England, the foreign became familiar and the familiar became foreign. My sense of who I was, along with my knowledge of the world, was constantly changing.

Perhaps you too have experienced feeling foreign in your own culture. In the company of strangers, you might feel a sense of familiarity. The experience of what feels foreign and what feels familiar undergoes a metamorphosis the more you engage with different cultures and languages.

Going with the flow

After graduating with a bachelor's degree in English, my love of language led me to pursue a master's degree in simultaneous interpreting. Simultaneous interpreting is when you interpret what a speaker is saying at the same time that the speaker is speaking. Given my love of English and my sensitivity to language, the choice seemed natural. I knew the work would come with its challenges, but I imagined all the fun I would have embracing them.

It turned out I was both right and wrong. I enjoyed the feeling of cocooning myself in a booth (a small room equipped for interpretation) and focusing entirely on the task. When I put my headphones on, it felt like the outside world was disappearing around me. I listened intently to Chinese phrases and interpreted them into English. When I did that, my worries washed away.

The psychologist Mihaly Csikszentmihalyi calls that state of mind a state of *flow*. To reach a state of flow, Csikszentmihalyi suggests you concentrate on a challenging activity that you have a high degree of skill in. But the activity can't pose too overwhelming of a challenge.[18] For example, a talented pianist might reach a state of flow when she plays Mozart's Piano Sonata No. 4 in E-flat major, a piece she has practiced many times over. But if she were to begin playing Beethoven's "Moonlight Sonata," it might take a few days or weeks of practice to reach the same state of flow. A soccer player might experience flow when he faces the challenges of a competitive game. Years of training has prepared him for the challenge, and that enables him to enter a flow state. Like the pro soccer player or the talented pianist, I found that if I concentrated intensely on interpreting, I too entered a state of flow. It felt like my sense of a separate self was fading away. I lost myself in the simultaneous act of listening to words in one language and giving them a new life in another.

Rather than lead me into a state of ecstasy, my experience of flow brought me a deep feeling of peace. But within that overriding sense of peace, I occasionally felt a little unsettled and bewildered. For one, I found myself mystified by how quickly my brain adapted to processing and reorganizing information, an act that in itself can disorientate anyone.

To understand all the mental acrobatics I did when interpreting, it's helpful to see how both English and Chinese convey meaning using their own logical sequencing and patterns of word configuration. The ways that Chinese and English arrange words and phrases, or order discrete units of meaning, differ dramatically. Telling a story in English from the original Chinese alters the manner and order in which you tell it. That can be challenging when you're listening to one language, which follows one path of logic, and you're speaking in another language, which follows a separate logic. Because of the lack of congruity between the English and Chinese, I had to continually arrange and rearrange discrete units of meaning to make sense of what the Chinese speaker was saying to the English audience. If I waited too long to interpret a particular phrase, I'd have to commit it to memory while the speaker continued speaking.

Immersing myself in simultaneous interpretation gave me insights into how language affects the way we think. When I delivered a presentation in two languages—Chinese and English—each presentation would follow a path of logic divergent from the other. If you're bilingual, speaking two languages activates different regions in your brain. Your mother tongue affects how you speak a second language, and speaking a foreign language influences the way you speak your mother tongue.

Despite my skills of interpreting, I still had the feeling that language itself was in some way inadequate. I began to grow aware of how poorly Chinese words conveyed what I wished to say. As Jacques Derrida writes in *Monolingualism of the Other,* "I have but one language, and yet it is not mine." [19] There were times when phrases came more naturally to me in English than in Chinese. English words flowed effortlessly off my tongue; in Chinese, my words fumbled. Words and phrases like "outliers," "achievers," "innermost value," "identity" and "integrity" do not have ready equivalents in Chinese. To express the ideas behind each of those phrases might require a whole sentence in Chinese. But the problem lies not in Chinese vocabulary or the patterns and rules of the Chinese language. My sense that words were inadequate hinted at something happening beneath the surface of words.

Language is more than we think it is. It's not merely a tool that we use passively to communicate. If you consider human beings as subjects who act upon a passive world, it's easy to mistake language as our instrument. But language also acts upon us. It can open our eyes and blind us; it can lead us to new opportunities or limit us. When you develop greater awareness of the possibilities within language, you can apply its wisdom. You can widen your peripheral vision and take in the horizon in a way you hadn't before.

Appreciating life

I've devoted my life to the study of language. Language has in return enriched who I am. It has given new frames of reference. It has enabled me to stay curious about the world. Attention to language has enhanced my attention for all of life. Through the study of language, I've grown more open-minded. I feel more comfortable expressing my own feelings. I pay greater attention to the feelings of others. I have a higher degree of patience for people and behaviors I don't have the capacity to understand.

I've also found that investigating the feelings behind words allows me to be patient with others. I've remained curious how both emotion and language drive human behavior. That helps me remain tolerant, empathetic, and compassionate toward others, both within and outside of my own culture.

Learning a second language has also taught me valuable lessons about myself. It led me to pursue a PhD in applied linguistics and language education. I've also since developed a keen interest in the study of neuroscience. By studying the brain, I've come to appreciate how significantly language influences the neural networks that affect our experiences of life and shape who we are.

Throughout my years of university teaching, students have regularly told me that language is only a tool for communication, not a means to self-awareness. To demonstrate how deeply the study of language has changed me, how intimately it entwines with the act of living, how it shapes so intricately my sense of meaning and informs my sense of purpose, I've had no choice but to write this book. The intricate beauty, innate potential, and immense power of language may already fill volumes in countless libraries around the world. But there's always more to learn. There's always new forms of language to study. Language is all around us. It delivers the news, envelopes us in ideas, and serenades us in songs. So deeply do we all live in language that few of us are entirely aware of its hold on us.

This book is an ode to language. It's also an ode to you. It's a testament to all that's possible when you embrace the power of language. I hope you enjoy the journey.

In Summary

For more than two decades, I have been learning English as a second language and working with it closely. My experience with English prompted my discovery of the power of language. This chapter is about my journey with the English language, what English learning has brought to me, and how they shaped my understanding of the power of language through a second language lens.

So, what did my journey with the English language look like?

- In my teenage years, I used English as a weapon in defence. A new person leaped out of me, who was confident, self-assured, and enthusiastic.
- When I lived in England, the experience of what feels foreign and what feels familiar was continually changing. It was a process of exploring the self and the other.
- I did a Master's program in simultaneous interpreting. Doing simultaneous interpreting sensitized me to the differences between the two languages and how they denote something deeper beneath the surface of words.

Next, what did English learning bring to me?

- It gave me new frames of reference, and I've grown more open-minded.
- It helped me remain tolerant, empathetic, and compassionate toward others.
- It has enriched me.

Finally, what have I understood of language through the lens of learning a second language?

- We live in language like fish in the water. Language is not only a tool for communication. It acts upon us.
- Language has the power to transform how you see the world and yourself.
- Language can shape how you experience reality and thus, the direction of your life.

Part 2

The Language Code: Lesser-known Secrets that Introduce You to a New World and a New Life

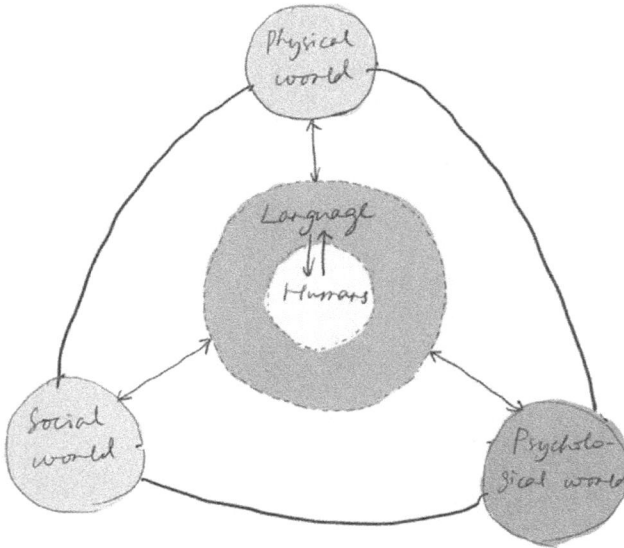

Figure 3

The above diagram (*figure 3*) displays how language shapes the way we experience reality—our physical, social, and psychological worlds. It plays a vital role in the way we think, live, and learn. In this part, the four chapters crack the language code and help you grow into a more profound understanding of language, opening your world to new horizons and preparing you for a new life.

Chapter 3: The World of Words Creates the World of Things

"Language is very powerful. Language does not just describe reality. Language creates the reality it describes."

Desmond Tutu[20]

"The world we see is defined and given meaning by the words we choose."

Ludwig Wittgenstein[21]

W e all use words to get our message across. Whether we want someone to pass the salt or to share her feelings, we rely on language to communicate. But many species communicate without language. When your puppy wags his tail when you walk in the door, he's telling you he's happy to see you. When he looks longingly at the slice of pizza you're eating for lunch, he's likely asking for a piece of it. Dog owners know that their canine companions communicate in manifold ways. Barks, howls, and whimpers—not to mention physical gestures—convey a whole gamut of canine emotions and needs. But the ways that dogs speak differ significantly from the ways that humans do.

The messages that animals send tend to be concrete rather than complex. They arise more from nature than nurture, embedded more in biology than culture. Humans too can send simple, concrete messages. But with our access to an intricate system of symbolic codes, a range of phonemes and a collection of letters and characters, we have the ability to convey complex ideas and feelings that dogs can't. With language, we can express intangible ideas and complex plans and theories. Humans use language to ask another person to "pass the salt," but we also use it to deliver lectures on the theory of relativity and negotiate ambiguous feelings about the government. Your dog might be able to hash a plan to steal your peanut butter sandwich from the kitchen counter, but he lacks the means to articulate that plan to other dogs in the neighborhood. You, on the other hand, can draw a map, write a manifesto, or send text messages—to whomever you wish and on whatever subject you desire.

As a human with access to language, you have at your disposal more than a mere tool to communicate. You can name the stars and identify patterns among them. You can observe a planet's place in the night sky and create myths around imagined characters in the cosmos. Through the magic of language, you can create and collaborate, dictate and describe, theorize and empathize. You can use words to imagine what it might have been like to be a paleolithic man 2.5 million years ago, an investment banker on Wall Street two decades ago, or an alien planting flowers in the Andromeda galaxy. You have the ability to sympathize with what's happening in others' minds and hearts. No matter how unfamiliar individuals might appear to you—culturally, socially or professionally—you can sense, through language, what it might be like to walk a mile in their shoes. Words can help you understand the frustrations, devastations and desperations of another gender, nationality, or faith. They can reveal dimensions of experience otherwise unknown to you.

Using finite words and characters, you can also create infinite messages and meanings. You can use language to intoxicate, enchant, and bewitch. You can use it to clarify, convey and comprehend. Your grasp of a particular language can transform how you interpret the world. Learning a new language invites you into another universe, another way of interpreting what you see, hear, and feel.

As a linguist, I've spent my career studying the science that attempts to explain the system of relationships between the forms and meanings of words. With any luck, my fellow linguists and I shed a little light on what otherwise might be incomprehensible to the untrained eye. But the systems of language are as complex and often as mysterious as the systems of stars. Not even Noam Chomsky has a complete grasp on them. As you learn about language through this book, consider yourself an explorer, discovering new things about yourself and the world.

Unlocking the codes

Like other primates—lemurs, marmosets, and monkeys—we have hands and feet and forward-looking eyes. But the ability to articulate ideas and feelings through speech—to use words to convey abstract reasoning and complicated emotions—sets us apart from our fellow monkeys. Understandably, scientists have been baffled by the evolution of language. What brought us from the primal grunt of a homo erectus to the soliloquy of Shakespeare? Few, if any, reliable documents exist on the matter. The consensus has commonly been that evolutionary adaption brought language into being. As the Earth's ecology responded to drastic environmental changes, homo sapiens put their heads and hands together to survive. They learned how to hunt, and later, to plant. They crafted tools to defend themselves and built shelters to protect their families from the wind and the rain. When life got more complex, it demanded increasingly sophisticated forms of speech. And so, the theory goes, came language.

Emerging from the human will to survive—as well as the longing to share feelings and ideas—distinct languages were born from the needs of core cultural groups. The proliferation of languages around the world reflects the diversity of cultures, tribes, and communities. The most extensive catalogue of the world's languages—*Ethnologue* (published by SIL International)— tells us that in 2009 there were 6,909 living languages.[22] Just as each continent comes with its own ecosystem of flora and fauna, each culture comes with its own ecosystem of words and meanings.

Australians, for example, have their own vocabulary to describe plants, animals and environmental phenomena specific to the Australian continent. Just as "blue banksia" grows only in Queensland, distinct words and phrases originate from specific regions. The word "bush" has a symbolic meaning to Australians. To describe the land, bush means a dry, mostly grassless wooded area with more shrubs than trees. But when Australians say, "he's gone to the bush," they mean that person has left for the remoteness of the wilderness and is distancing himself from civilization.

The words for specific colors have their own regional varieties, too. Many people think our perception of color is an objective fact. But different languages represent colors in different ways. Take the color blue. In Russian, no single word exists for blue; instead, Russian has words for light blue and dark blue. Japanese, Thai, and Korean use the same word to describe blue and green. Historically, language, literature, and art adopted the color blue long after the adoption of red, black, brown, ochre, pink, and purple. Across cultures and throughout the centuries, blue has represented everything from poverty to piety to nobility—all depending on the context.

We also like to think of the five senses as objective, universal phenomena. But both culture and language influence sensory perception. How each group of people sees, hears, smells, tastes, and feels arises from biology. But each also arises from the training of attention, which can be culturally specific. In Nijmegen, the Netherlands, a team of anthropologists and psychologists at the Max Planck Institute for Psycholinguistics and Radboud University discovered that while Americans struggle to identify scents, the people of the rainforest in the Malay Peninsula can name individual scents with alarming accuracy. Cultures around the world use their own metaphors to describe sound, and those metaphors can be powerful enough to disrupt how people perceive reality.[23] The physical landscape also influences our perception. If you spend long enough in Florence, writes Stanford professor of anthropology T.M. Luhrmann, you begin to see colors you have never seen before because of the way that the "soft light moves across the ochre buildings."[24]

The variety of vocabulary across cultures extends beyond that which describe the sensual world. Every language has nouns (to identify subjects and objects), verbs (to indicate the actions taken by or related to the subjects and objects) and adjectives and adverbs (to describe the qualities of nouns and verbs). Those parts of speech represent how we see and experience the physical world. In Spanish and French, nouns have two genders: feminine and masculine. In German, there are three—one of them is neuter. In English and Chinese, nouns have no gender. In German, the word "bridge" is feminine; in Spanish and French, it is masculine. Lera Boroditsky, an assistant psychology professor at Stanford University, reported in a 2009 article the findings of an experiment she conducted where she asked participants to describe the image that came to them when they read the word "bridge." The words that came to mind for the German participants were "elegant" and "beautiful." The Spanish and French participants used traditionally masculine words like "big," "strong," and "towering."[25]

Why do specific languages ascribe gender to words? Does a culture's choice of gender for specific nouns reflect that culture's relationship to the physical word? Might those choices tell us how people understand their social world?

Language: Our narrator, our navigator

The diversity of habitats across the globe helps to explain the variety of ways people speak. When humans experience environmental phenomena—droughts, monsoons, and seasonal transitions—they often develop collective practices to explain, cope with, and create meaning from them. For example, in the Northern Hemisphere, the winter solstice—the shortest day of the year—falls around the 21st of December. Around that time, the Earth's north pole tilts the farthest away from the Sun. Neolithic people of England and Ireland marked the end of autumn and the beginning of winter with the winter solstice. When the winter solstice ends, a new year begins. A number of religious celebrations—Christmas and Hanukkah, for example—fall around the 21st of December. In the southern hemisphere in Thailand, the seasons follow a different pattern. Songkran, or the Thai New Year, begins in mid-April. The word "Songkran" comes from a Sanskrit word that means "astrological passage." For Thais, mid-April marks a time of transformation and change. Both cultures—European and Thai—derive meaning from the movement of the Sun. Both have developed cultural festivals to represent, celebrate and understand astrological and environmental phenomena.

Language, suggests Professor of Language and Education Alistair Pennycook, does not only give names to the seasons, it is "a central organizing activity of social life."[26] Rather than view language as a concrete system, one that we impose upon the environment, Pennycook views language as an act that we perform within an environment. Language is a process of communicating, but it's also a product of communication. Pennycook sees language as an act that entwines with the social life of a specific geographical location. Language, he suggests, cannot exist outside of its context.

But how do different languages "act" within a culture? Consider how two cultures use language to describe one of the most basic units of social life—the family. Both English and Chinese have words for "uncle." In English, your uncle might be the brother of your father or mother, or the husband of your aunt. But in Chinese, several words exist for "uncle." There is a word for the elder brother of your father (伯父 *bofu*), another for the younger brother of your father (叔父 *shufu*), one for the elder brother of your mother (舅舅 *jiujiu*), and yet another for the younger brother of your mother (舅妈 *jiuma*). The list does not stop there. The Chinese use a different name for the husband of their aunts. To confuse things further, "aunt" can refer to any number of women in the family in China. Translators often find themselves at a loss when choosing the best word in Chinese to replace either "uncle" or "aunt." To add to the confusion, words for aunt and uncle multiply when you start to refer to your second or third generation relatives. Even I get confused.

Why are there so many words for uncle and aunt in Chinese? Sociologist and anthropologist Xiaotong Fei points out that social relations affect every dimension of Chinese culture, including its language. Traditional hierarchies influence how people address one another. Family members hold rank according to their age. Older generations hold a higher place on the ladder than younger generations. Outside the family, the degree of authority people hold determines their social status. Fei notes that the Chinese sense of hierarchy extends not only vertically through a social structure, but horizontally across it, like waves of water rippling outward in a pond. Around each member of society exists concentric social networks. To distinguish between the two dimensions of social hierarchy, Fei uses the phrase "differential pattern" (差序格局 *chaxugeju*).[27]

"Differential pattern" may sound like a little opaque. But think of it this way. Chinese people rely on a pattern that defines how they address people, especially their kin. In China we also use the word "uncle" to address a stranger who is around our parents' age and who we're meeting for the first time. The term "uncle" shows respect for a man of an older generation. But more importantly, we use the title "uncle" to help us maintain appropriate distance and proper etiquette. Chinese culture attaches a great deal of significance to all social relationships. Using specific titles for different people helps us to navigate those relationships.

Beyond its influence on relationships within your family and social network, language also affects the way you express your feelings. In English, words that describe laughter are often direct and straightforward. When you hear the words "cackle," "chuckle," "guffaw" and "roar," you can almost see the facial expressions and hear the sounds of the person who is cackling, chuckling, guffawing, or roaring. Cackle, chuckle, guffaw, and roar are all *onomatopoeic*; they sound like the thing they are naming. The word "cackle" alludes to the raucous cry of a hen after laying an egg. When someone "chuckles," she quietly suppresses her laughter. To "guffaw" means to burst out in a loud hearty laugh. If you "roar," you laugh unrestrainedly, like a wild animal.

In Chinese, phrases that describe laughter are most often indirect and abstract. In Chinese, we have words that describe the degree of laughter, like a "slight laugh" or a "soft smile" 莞尔 wan'er or 微笑 weixiao). We have also have the expression belly "laugh" to describe laughter that is so loud and wild that you hold your belly (捧腹大笑 pengfudaxiao). But Chinese expressions for laughter don't, like their English equivalents, trigger images of hens and wild animals. Instead, Chinese words for laughter tend to arouse senses or feelings. The Chinese word "开怀一笑" means to laugh heartedly; "冷笑 lengxiao" means to smile coldly; "苦笑 kuxiao" means to smile bitterly; "傻笑 shajiao" means to smile foolishly; and "奸笑 jianxiao" means to smile in a sinister way. Each of those phrases implies a discrete social judgment of whoever is "laughing."

All those differences between the two languages also implies subtle differences between the two cultures. Both English and Chinese negotiate and regulate social interaction in their own ways. Each has its own codes. Most often, language embodies those codes. No two cultures perceive the expression of emotion in exactly the same way. Since the Chinese and English have their own mores, traditions, and biases, the words each culture uses to describe an outburst or suppression of laughter reveals the psychology of each culture. If you're accustomed to describing laughter as "smiling coldly" or "smiling bitterly," you're more likely to keep a distance from whoever is "laughing" in that manner.

Language: The blood of the soul

"Language is the blood of the soul into which thoughts run and out of which they grow."

Oliver Wendell Holmes[28]

Every house has a frame—a structure that supports it. Every human has a skeleton—an internal framework of bone and cartilage that holds us up and governs her range of motion. In linguistics, a frame describes a structural environment that directs how a language uses words and phrases. That frame might be an underlying grammar. It might be a social context. The frame of your language and your culture influences how you interpret laughter, how you see the color blue and how you address your aunts and uncles. Even though you are not consciously aware of it, grammar dictates how you interpret the world. Different rules of grammar apply to each language; different structures of language determine how we use clauses, phrases, and words.

To understand the way that grammar structures language, think of the influence of technology on your day-to-day life. Most of us now live in the world of digital technology. We've grown familiar with its rules, platforms, and social contexts. For those who can code, technology has its own language governed by its own grammar. If you use a mobile device frequently, it will influence how you learn, connect, and communicate. Social apps such as Facebook, Twitter, and WeChat have changed how we keep up with family and friends. Tinder and Bumble have transformed how we meet people. GPS has altered the way we travel from one point to another.

To acquire or adopt digital technology means to submit to a new framework. If you depend on that framework every day—to work, to gather information, to socialize—it will structure how you experience and interact with the world. When technology becomes indispensable, it begins to organize the way we live our lives. Adopting or acquiring language has the same effect.

Since each language has its own framework, learning a new one demands that you adopt an entirely new set of rules. You must organize and articulate your thoughts in entirely new ways. For adults who have already grown accustomed to one set of rules, submitting to another will pose challenges to their habitual ways of thinking. You learned in chapter one how Chinese and English have remarkably different frameworks. English arranges units of speech like an engineer designs a train: compartments and carriages are clearly connected. Like a train following its tracks, English moves in a linear fashion.

But Chinese organizes words and phrases like an umbrella with radiating spokes. Units of language, like radiating spokes, connect clearly to one point—a central idea. But the connection between two sentences or spokes is often ambiguous and hard to trace. In Chinese, it makes perfect sense to say, "The rain fell; the river flooded; the house washed away", which sounds to be poorly constructed with a loose connection between different meaning units. Unlike English, which demands explicit grammatical links among units of speech, Chinese makes no clear logical links on the surface. The links are embedded in the meanings underlying the words. Chinese speakers reach an understanding of a text or a speech by situating its phrases within a context.

Although Chinese has connectives, ("and" and "but") and discourse markers, (words and phrases such as "well" or "I mean" whose function is to organize speech into segments), it relies on the implicit links reflected in the meanings behind the words. Where English makes connections explicitly—on the surface of speech—Chinese makes them tacitly—below the surface.

Those unfamiliar with Chinese may make the mistake of assuming that Chinese people are lacking in logic. When English speakers listen to a Chinese speech through an interpreter, they can easily lose sight of connections if the interpreter fails to add explicit grammatical links and discourse markers. When I speak English, my students say that I speak more logically than I do in Chinese. Those two ways of speaking—explicitly and implicitly—point to two ways of thinking.

A matter of tense

To add to all the differences between English and Chinese, English has several forms—or tenses—of verbs. Take the verb "play." Like any verb, "play" takes on several tenses depending on the context. You can say "I play with my puppy" if you want to communicate that you play with him every day. If you're playing right now, you'd say: "I am playing with my puppy." If you were playing with him yesterday, you might say: "I was playing with my puppy," "I played with my puppy," or "I have been playing with my puppy." You can talk about the possibility of play or its conditions: "I might play with my puppy" or "I could have been playing with my puppy." You can also communicate your future plans for play: "I am going to play with my puppy."

But in Chinese, there are no tenses. If you're used to using tenses, you might find it hard to imagine life without them. How do you speak about the past or write about the future if there are no tenses? In Chinese, when we speak about something that happened in the past, we often mention when that event took place at the beginning of the story. We use the present tense for every action that follows. When we describe something that might happen in the future, we use the same tactic. We mention the time frame. In Chinese, we say: "I play today," "I play yesterday," or "I play tomorrow." The verb "play" stays the same, but the time indicators change.

In English, tense usage is often not straightforward and linear. For effect, writers often switch tenses strategically. They might use the past tense to describe the future or the present to describe the past. Take Fergal Keane's letter to his newborn son, Daniel, which the BBC broadcast in 1996 on its radio program, "From Our Own Correspondent."[29] Keane begins his letter with simple present tense: "It is six o'clock in the morning," he writes, "you are asleep cradled in my left arm." He moves to the present perfect to describe the effect that his baby has had on his day-to-day life: "Days have melted into night and back again," he writes, "…your coming has turned me upside down and inside out." He uses the metaphor of language to illustrate the experience: "We are learning a new grammar." He switches tenses again—from the perfect to the progressive. He describes his days as "a long sentence whose punctuation marks are feeding and winding and nappy changing."

When Keane writes about what he's witnessed as a foreign correspondent in Afghanistan, Rwanda, and Eritrea, he moves to the past tense. But when he shares a personal story of hardships within his own family, he returns to present: "It begins thirty-five years ago in a big city on a January morning with snow on the ground and a woman walking to the hospital to have her first baby." Keane is describing the day of his own birth. That story from "long ago" is also a story about his parents. Phrases like "long lines of blood and family" give the impression that the story of his family extends far back into the past and stretches far into the future. It is not a story solely about himself, but "about our lives," he writes, "and how we can get lost in them." "Our lives"—meaning all human lives—follow mythic patterns, ones that Daniel, his son, will come to recognize. The journey of getting lost and finding your way back again is a journey that transcends any single individual. It transcends time.

When Keane writes about his father, he locates the story clearly in the past: "the cancer of alcoholism ate away at the man and he lost his family." But when he addresses his son, he speaks to the boy in the present: "When you are older, my son, you will learn about how complicated life becomes, how we can lose our way."

If I were to translate those paragraphs into Chinese, there would be no change of tense at all. Tense is simply untranslatable in a tenseless language. Would a Chinese reader interpret Keane's letter differently than an English reader? It depends. An English reader might find Keane's use of present tense engaging; it might enable her to visualize the story more readily. When Keane uses the past tense to describe his father, an English reader might understand that the trials and tribulations of the writer's father have ended. Although a Chinese reader wouldn't experience the effects of a change of verb tense when reading, a good translator can convey the effect the writer conveys in other ways.

Given that the Chinese language stays in the present tense, is it easier for Chinese people to remain in the present moment? If, grammatically speaking, the past, present and future exist as one tense in Chinese, does that affect how Chinese people think about the past and future?

When I speak in English, I often need to remain conscious of tense. If I don't, I may make the mistake of using the present tense to refer to something that happened in the past or in the future. That was especially true for me when I was first learning English. My mother tongue interfered. As I developed fluency, my first language interfered less. But I began to notice how when I focused on using the correct tense in English, I began to perceive events in time in subtly different ways. I began to see past events as detached from the present. That alleviated some of the sadness that I had associated with painful memories. It also made bad omens feel less intimidating. When I speak Chinese, the past and the future feel more closely connected with the present. In Chinese, sad memories feel more poignant and bad omens more foreboding.

A study conducted by the Chinese American economist Keith Chen suggests that I am not alone in those perceptions. Chen compared the spending behaviors of people living in the 35 countries that make up the Organization for Economic Cooperation and Development (OECD). He found that those who speak a language without a future tense view the future as bearing immediate effect on the present.

Since the future feels present, they are more inclined to save money for it. But those who speak a language with a future tense tend to see the future as further removed from the present, so they feel less inclined to save money. Chen discovered that those "pockets of futureless language speakers all around the world turn out to be, by and large, some of the world's best savers." They save "an average difference of 5% of GDP" per year. To Chen, the theory applies not only to the ability to save, but to anything related to the future. "Futureless language speakers," he writes, are more likely to be aware of how smoking affects their long-term health and how overeating leads to obesity.[30] Interestingly, some people have vehemently attacked Keith Chen's study of the ways that language affects financial planning. But when they ran the data themselves, they got the same results.

If all that is true, does the language we speak affect our ability to delay gratification? You might be familiar with the Stanford marshmallow experiment, a study originally led by the psychologist Walter Mischel in 1972. In the experiment, a researcher gave a child a marshmallow and offered him a choice: Eat the marshmallow now or wait until an adult comes back with an additional treat to enjoy. Follow-up studies demonstrated that the children who resisted the temptation to eat the marshmallow scored higher on scholastic achievement tests and maintained a healthier body mass index in adulthood.

Later variations on the marshmallow experiment suggest that myriad factors, not only will power, influence a child's ability to resist temptation and delay gratification. When conducted in Germany and Cameroon, test results indicated that cultural upbringing affects outcomes. Cameroonian children exhibited more self-regulation.[31] Was it the hierarchal parenting style in Cameroon, one that expects obedience and respect, that led children to execute more emotional self-regulation? Or was it the hands-on breast-feeding style of Cameroonian mothers that influenced how children in the experiment experienced desire and gratification? Research in China suggests that kids who tend to trust people overall are more willing to wait longer for a reward. But does language play a role in how long kids wait to eat a marshmallow?

In 2009, students from Shanghai topped international rankings in scholastic achievement.[32] Statistically, Chinese students outperform Americans in math scores. Do those statistics reflect the Chinese language or its culture? Or both? In her 2017 book *Little Soldiers*, Lenora Chu, an American of Chinese descent living in Shanghai, unearths some of the cultural differences underpinning the outstanding academic success amongst the Chinese. While it's a Chinese tradition to invest in education, both financially and psychologically, some of the cultural differences that contribute to academic success are deeply embedded in the language.[33] Language encodes the customs, perspectives, and values of any culture. It constructs and is constructed by culture. It guides individual behavior within any social context.

Further studies have illustrated how language affects our perspective of time, and by virtue of that, how it influences how we think and live. In *A Sideways Look at Time*, British author Jay Griffiths writes about dimensions of time experienced in different cultures around the world. The Karen, a hill-tribe in the forests of Northern Thailand, do not rely on a clock for their sense of time. They tell the time by the quality of air in the forest. In the morning, the air is thin and damp. In the evening, it's thickened by steam and smoke. The Karen describe how far they are from both the sunset and their home using the same phrase. Time and distance are connected in their language. The phrase *diyi ba* literally means "not far away."[34]

Most modern languages measure time with a clock, chronologically from hour to hour and one day to the next. The clock defines the length of our workdays; it calculates the start and end of each rush hour; and it dictates our deadlines. But the Karen use *Kairological* time, a system that measures an alternative sense of both the hours and their movement. *Kairological* time is defined by nature—the air in the forest and the arrival of dusk. For the Karen, there's neither a need to rush nor to stress over deadlines because, just as there's always distance between you and the sunset, there's always time. The future is not a concept the Karen know well. They strive less toward future goals. Their future comes to them and recedes behind them. It's as though the Karen always stand still in a place called "the present." They live in the here and now. For them, the present is eternal. The Chinese language may not have tenses, but it does have words for the past and the future, which give the Chinese a sense of the passing of time that differs from the Karen.

Undoubtedly, the language we speak affects our sense of time. How we experience time influences how we think, feel, and act. Our perception of time has a profound impact on how we live our lives.

Nouns: The building blocks

Nouns are small but important building blocks of language. In English, there are two types of nouns: countable and uncountable. The word "bread" is uncountable, but "scone" is countable. "Cake" can be either countable or uncountable. Rice is uncountable. A child brought up speaking English in the United Kingdom doesn't give much thought to why nouns are either countable or uncountable just as French speakers tend not to give much thought to why a noun is feminine or masculine. But for a Chinese learner of English, the concept of countable and uncountable nouns can be difficult to grasp. All Chinese nouns—whether they refer to people, places or things—can be counted. In Chinese, you can always count bread, rice, or cake. In Chinese, you can say: "I ate two breads today" or "there is a rice on his lip."

After living in the UK for a while, I began to understand why bread might be an uncountable noun in English. In England, you eat bread by the slice or by the piece. It's unlikely that you would devour a whole loaf of bread at once. In China, baking is a Western activity, and Chinese shops always sell bread in a bag. The most common type of bread in China comes in round shapes of medium size (one bread is usually one portion for an adult). Chinese people usually say: "I eat one bread this morning." But we use the same grammar to describe eating rice. Rice is usually eaten by the bowl. In English, the noun "rice" is uncountable. There are too many grains of rice in a bowl to count even if you wanted to. If you want to refer to a single rice, in English you would say "a grain of rice."

Eating constitutes one of the most important social practices in any culture. You can find the traces of a culture's eating habits embedded in its language. English speakers tend to have two senses of the quantity of one food: the macro and the micro, or the whole and the part. In English, you can have a piece of bread, a loaf of bread, or just bread. In English, there's rice and then there's a grain of rice, a bowl of rice, and a bag of rice. In Chinese, every noun can be counted individually. That might explain why Chinese excel in math. Our love for numbers may come from our ability to count anything!

But that love of numbers goes beyond statistics and measurements, beyond quantifying what in some languages is unquantifiable. Chinese culture also has a 4,000-year-old tradition of numerology, or the belief that certain numbers are auspicious and others inauspicious. In Western culture, the number seven is often considered a "lucky number." There are seven days of the week, seven notes on a musical scale, and seven colors in a rainbow. In the Bible, God made the world in six days and rested on the seventh. But in China, the seventh month of the year is a "ghost month." The word for seven in Mandarin sounds like the word for "deceive," which can only make it unlucky. Eight, however, sounds like the Cantonese verb "to prosper." The 2008 Summer Olympics in Beijing began on the eighth day of the eighth month at eight minutes and eight seconds past eight p.m. local time. Sichuan Airlines bought the phone number +86 28 8888 8888 for approximately $280,000 in 2003.

Who are we without our words?

Language influences our psychological, physical, and social experience. It shapes our experience of reality. The French psychoanalyst and psychiatrist Jacques Lacan expresses it this way: "It is the world of words which creates the world of things."[35] The way we create "the world of things" with our "world of words" differs depending on which "world of words," or which language, we live in. Every language has its own sense, its own shape, and its own character. The German language, just like German-made automobiles, has rigor and order. In comparison to Chinese, German requires more information to construct a sentence. You have to know the gender of people and things and who are driving the action. French, with its clarity and lucidity and in terms of how words follow the thought, is known as the language of diplomacy. English, because of its openness and compatibility, might be the language of literature. These features reveal a lot about the people behind the languages, about who we are. Speaking a language is therefore "a form of life," as Ludwig Wittgenstein put it, and it is essential to our identities as individuals and as a species.[36]

Practice building awareness and compassion communication to achieve personal and professional goals

If language and culture affect how you experience and represent the world, how can you use that knowledge to your benefit? For one, having a more intimate awareness of language can improve how you communicate with people from another culture. That awareness can help you understand people better from other cultures. It can also help you understand your own culture. It is easy to take things in our own culture for granted. By exposing yourself to another language and another culture, you experience new ways of thinking and acting.

For example, in the West, when people talk on the phones to their family, they often end the conversation with "love you." In Asian cultures, it's hard to imagine. In China, love is rarely expressed explicitly in words, even for couples madly in love. Couples might say, "I love you" occasionally, but they would never end every conversation with it. As someone who grew up in Asia, I sometimes wonder if expressing "love you" frequently in everyday life diminishes the impact of those words. But I also wonder if Asian cultures might benefit from more explicitly expressing love to keep love alive.

By understanding your culture and its customs, you can gain a richer understanding of yourself. If you know that the words you use shape how you experience life, you can choose your words carefully and gain greater control over your own thoughts, feelings and behaviors. For example, as an Asian, you can learn to use "I love you," or similar expressions, more often with your families to cultivate healthier thoughts about loving and being loved. For a Westerner, instead of saying "I love you," you can try using other words that demonstrate care and affection. You might say "I care about you" or "I appreciate you." You can share with a loved one what you love about them or demonstrate love through your actions. In many cases, that might make more of an impact on someone than hearing the words "I love you."

That approach to love is one example of how you can make the familiar unfamiliar. Questioning your use of familiar words or changing how you express your feelings can give you a fresh perspective on them. In the context of cross-cultural communication, it can act as a guiding principle.

Here are further tips to making the familiar unfamiliar and the unfamiliar familiar.

1. Take a slow stretch and yawn deeply. You might not feel like yawning, but if you fake three or four yawns, eventually you will get a real one. According to research in neuroscience, yawning is the fastest way to eliminate neurological stress.[37] It interrupts the noise in your head and enables you to shift your state of mind in as fast as a few seconds. In other words, it helps deeply relax your body. When your body is relaxed, your mind is relaxed. That's when intuition, creativity and "Aha" moments come more readily.

2. Focus first on familiar words or phrases, and then repeat the process with unfamiliar words or phrases. Close your eyes and take ten seconds to allow associations with the word or phrase to arise in your mind. Keeping your eyes closed will help you access your intuition and creativity much faster. To make the familiar unfamiliar, ask yourself the question: "If I were to explain this to a three-year-old child, what would I say?" To make unfamiliar familiar, you can ask

yourself: "In what context is this spoken?", "Why does the speaker say this and what effect does he want to achieve?" and "What other things did the speaker say that echo the meaning of this word or phrase?"

3. Consult dictionaries and play with words. For example, suppose an English and a Chinese person are conducting a business meeting. The Chinese person, translating an idea from the Chinese into English, might say: "It's interesting." This is a very simple expression in English. When the English people hear it, they might not take it seriously. English people might use the expression to dismiss an idea in a way that doesn't sound rude. But for a Chinese speaker, the word "interesting" might be closer to the dictionary definition "arousing curiosity and interest." If you look it up in a thesaurus, you might find "interesting" relates to "attentiveness," "inquisitiveness," "enjoyment," "delight," "attraction," "appeal," and "charm." And the list goes on. You can play with words and see how different associations arise from the process.

When you take these steps, you'll begin to see how malleable language can be and how our associations with it can change over time and with practice. When you learn to make the familiar unfamiliar and the unfamiliar familiar, it will improve your empathy with people from other cultures. It will help you to understand how their associations with words might be slightly different. That will inevitably improve your intercultural communication.

Besides this principle of making the familiar unfamiliar and the unfamiliar familiar, there are other tips that can help you achieve effective intercultural communication and communication in general:

1. Observe another person's body language.

Thirty percent of what we say is communicated nonverbally. When you're having a conversation, listen to the other person's words, but also listen to how those words are spoken. What gestures do you notice? How is your friend holding her shoulders? Where is she looking? If you observe carefully, you may gain greater empathy for the other person. You may also have a better understanding about the words he uses.

2. Speak slowly and briefly.

A fast speaker creates tension for her listeners. Human beings can only take in four to seven "chunks" of information at any one time. If you speak slowly and with fewer words, it not only helps release that tension, it helps your audience to hear what you are saying at a deeper level. Speaking with fewer words also helps you focus on your most important message. It reduces the chances that you'll be misunderstood.

3. Sport a slight smile and soften your eyes.

Wearing an expression of a slight smile and soft eyes will enable your audience to trust you more. Neurologically, when people look at an inviting and no-threatening facial expression, it creates what neuroscientists call neuro-resonance. When you have neuro-resonance, you'll resolve conflict before it begins. Your audience will more likely stay relaxed and share your peaceful state of mind.

But how do you sport a slight smile and soften your eyes?

It's impossible to do when you're tense and nervous. Before you enter a conversation, think about your innermost values. When you sense conflict arising, return to those values. That practice will ground you in what's most important and will relax you. The peace you feel in your heart will naturally soften your eyes and lift your mouth into a gentle smile.

4. Share your values and expectations.

When you share your values and expectations with another person, you'll find that most of the time, your values are similar, at least in some sense. For example, in a business meeting between executives of two companies, both parties will most likely value trust and respect. When you find you value similar things as another person, it's easy to agree on a way forward and get the most from a conversation. Meanwhile, it's important to communicate your expectations. I personally have experienced intercultural communication breakdown because expectations are misunderstood.

For example, when Chinese and English executives meet to sign a deal, there's always the possibility of a communication breakdown, but it can be difficult to see it coming. It's common that Chinese speakers assume that their expectations have been understood when they haven't. In Chinese language and culture, the context carries meaning, often more than the words themselves. Meaning is often implied. That can be difficult for English speakers to understand.

English speakers, on the other hand, use mild expressions to express denial and rejection. They might say, "This design still needs lots of work." What they mean is, "This design is not good enough." A Chinese speaker might misinterpret that and hear, "The design is fine, it's just that we need to do further work."

When Chinese people nod, it means that they get what you're saying. But it can be misunderstood as a sign of agreement. When it comes to signing a deal, both parties might find themselves surprised when a breakdown of communication happens. Neither was sensitive to the subtle differences in meaning conveyed.

5.   Make the best of cultural differences.

When people from different cultures come together for a meeting, they usually end the meeting with the distinct feeling of the cultural differences inherent in cross-cultural communication. If the meeting goes well, and if expectations are met, rather than let the differences create tension, they laugh about them.

When a deal goes badly or expectations aren't met, people often blame the differences in culture.

But differences of culture do not in themselves lead to failed outcomes. It's the way that people interpret those differences that makes all the difference. Sometimes, all it takes is a change of perspective. Cultural differences can work to your advantage. Just think of the times you have benefited from new ways of thinking and behaving. Sometimes taking a new path can lead to the most exciting results.

For example, the Chinese tend to be more risk-averse than Americans. But there are no right or wrong paths. We need both conservative views and progressive views, both caution and risk. We may need to find a path that integrates caution and risk.

These neurotips do not only apply to intercultural communication. They apply to any kind of communication. If you have a conversation with someone from the same cultural background, that person will no doubt be different from you. Sharing the same cultural background does not guarantee that you share similar behaviors. Sometimes social and economic backgrounds matter more than cultural backgrounds.

So, use these tips whenever you have a meeting or conversation with others.

In Summary

Human language is unique because it can refer to things that they are not present; it can create infinite messages and meanings with finite words and characters. Our lives are deeply entwined with the intellectual development of language. Through the magic of language, we accomplish every act of living. We use language to create, collaborate, dictate, and describe, theorize, and empathize. But language goes beyond these. In this chapter, the codes of language are unlocked in the following perspectives:

- Language across cultures represent how we see and experience the physical world. Examples include words of colors and genders/gender-less of nouns in different languages.
- Language reflects a culture's relationship to the social world, i.e., how people build social networks and express feelings. Examples include words for aunt, uncle and words for laugh in the Chinese and English language.
- Language is a frame that helps us structure, organize, and articulate thoughts in a particular way. It affects our mental world—our way of thinking and living. Examples include how English arranges units of speech like a train, and Chinese, an umbrella.
- Language shapes our experience of reality. It is essential to our identities as individuals and as a species.

To illustrate how language affects the way we think and live and how it shapes our experience of reality, I used tense and nouns specifically to explain and make my point. The following diagram (4) summarizes important ideas regarding these two aspects.

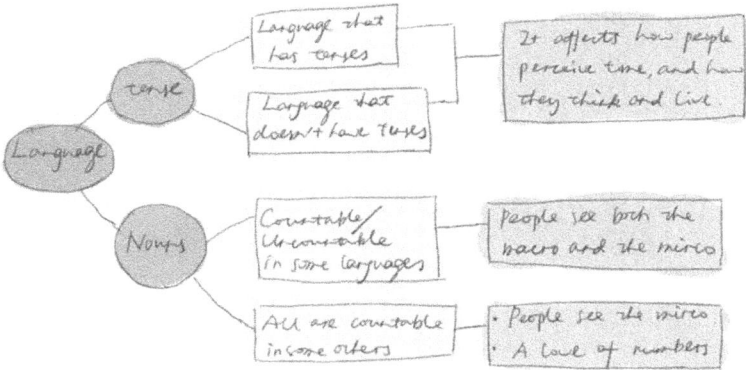

Figure 4

At the end of this chapter, I gave you tips for using the above knowledge to achieve effective intercultural communication and communication in general. Among these tips, making familiar unfamiliar and the unfamiliar familiar is especially emphasized. However, you can start with any advice that appeals to you and begin to practice it in your real-life conversations. When you think you have mastered the particular skills involved in that advice, you can come back and think about how you can use other tips as well.

Chapter 4: You're Neither Your Words Nor Your Thoughts

"The limits of my language are the limits of my world."

Ludwig Wittgenstein[38]

In the last chapter, we looked at the ways that language constructs our physical, social, and mental life and how that reveals who we are collectively as human beings. Taking a bird's eye view, we touched on how language defines a culture. But how does language define us as individuals? How does it shape the way each of us makes meaning?

First, let me ask you a question.

Do you remember how you learned your first language?

You don't have to be a linguist to answer that question. If you're reading this book, you've acquired a language. If you have children, you've seen how quickly they pick up a language—step by step, word by word. Noam Chomsky, one of the most influential linguists and cognitive scientists living today, believes that humans are born with the innate ability for language. Language is hardwired into our genetic programming. It distinguishes us from other animals.

But if language is encoded in our genes, how does the environment affect our capacity to learn language? How much of language comes by nature and how much by nurture? Perhaps the only way to answer that question is by studying children who have been isolated from human contact from a young age. As you might imagine, there are very few cases.

Victor of Aveyron, or Victor the Wild Boy, is one of them. If you're a fan of French cinema, you might be familiar with the 1970 film directed by François Truffaut, *L'enfant sauvage (The Wild Child)*, which is based on true events.

Around the turn of the 17th century, villagers in Southern France spotted a boy of around 12 running naked and wild in woods. Eventually captured, the "wild child" fell into the hands of a society of naturalists, physicians, historians, linguists, writers, and archaeologists who studied human behavior in relation to its environment. The *Société des observateurs de l'homme* (the Society of the Observers of Man), as they called themselves, were particularly interested in the development of children. They wondered if the wild boy was a "noble savage," a term that symbolized for them the innate goodness of a person uncorrupted by the influences of civilization. Or did the young boy live in what Thomas Hobbes called "the state of nature" (that is, an experience of life as "nasty, brutish, and short")? What makes a human being a human being?

Psychiatrists eventually diagnosed the wild child as an "incurable idiot." They decided the boy belonged to an insane asylum. Challenging that prognosis, a young medical student, Jean Marc Itard, offered to take the child home. He taught the boy to eat, eventually named him "Victor" and spent years training and teaching him. Itard believed that two things separated human beings from animals—their ability to use language and their capacity for empathy.

Under Itard, Victor learnt to spell out the words *lait* (milk) and *Oh, Dieu* (Oh, God). Although the young doctor didn't succeed in teaching the boy how to communicate his feelings through language, Victor expressed a capacity for empathy, most noticeably when he consoled the housemaid when she was weeping over her husband's death.

If language is indeed intrinsic to the human experience—as both Itard and Chomsky believe—and if the ability to speak is encoded in our genetic material, what stopped Victor of Aveyron from learning more words? Did the trauma he suffered rob him of his natural ability to speak? Or perhaps at the age of 12, Victor had already passed the critical period of brain development when children are most sensitive to language and therefore capable of quickly acquiring it.

Whatever the reason behind Victor's inability to fully integrate the use of language, Itard's observations support the hypothesis that humans develop speech both by their natural inclinations and through their interactions within a language-rich environment.

That theory might explain the range of abilities that young children demonstrate when it comes to language acquisition. Although all children have an innate ability for language, each child has been exposed to a different network of influences that affect how that child speaks. Just like most of us are born with a pair of lungs, not all of our lungs function at the same capacity. If you smoke a pack of cigarettes a day, your lungs will suffer for it. But if you exercise regularly in the fresh air, you'll condition your lungs to function at a higher capacity.

You may have noticed how kids pick up on the phrases used by their caregivers and friends. The way they speak usually reflects the impact of their environment. Dialects and accents are prime examples of this. A young girl who grows up in Belfast will speak English with a Northern Irish accent. If she grows up in Kentucky, she speaks with a Southern US accent. If she's born in Melbourne, she speaks with an Australian accent. If she is Irish, instead of asking "how are you?" she might say: "Bout ye?" Raised in America, she might say: "How y'all doing?" If Australian, she'll likely ask: "How you going?"

Each geographical milieu affects how we put sounds and syntax together. In the same way, a boy who grows up in a household of voracious readers will likely be exposed to a more extensive vocabulary than some of the other boys in his class. At the age of 18 months, some toddlers can speak in complete sentences. For others, it might take another year and a half. It's a commonly held belief that the more caregivers interact with a child and encourage that child to interact with others, the more that child will develop skills in language. Although adults are less sensitive to the language in their surroundings than children, the speed and ease in which adults learn a language increases the more they interact with it.

Whose words are you speaking?

If you accept that the words you use reflect the geography, culture, and milieu you live within, can you claim these words your own? And if they're not your words, whose words are they?

Like everyone, you were born to a mother and into a mother tongue. If you were born to an English mother and raised in an English household, your mother tongue is likely English. If you were born in Hong Kong and grew up speaking Cantonese, Cantonese is probably your mother tongue. If your Belgian parents raised you to speak Dutch, but you moved across an ocean and studied in Australia, Dutch is still your mother, or native, tongue.

Speaking your mother tongue often feels intimate, familiar and comfortable. The verb "to mother" means to demonstrate affection, care and protection. You feel at home when you feel safe to express yourself knowing that whoever is listening will understand you. That sense of safety disappears, naturally, when you've lost your way in a foreign country. It's never easy to struggle to remember the words to ask for directions back to your hotel when you are just learning the language. Speaking (or trying to speak) a new language under any circumstances often stirs up feelings of distance, discomfort, and doubt.

But is your mother tongue always comfortable and familiar? How much do you genuinely know your own language? Can you ever feel completely at home when you speak it? If you ask a linguist those questions, she likely won't give you straight answers. Linguists spend their careers studying the science and structure of language. But the more they study, the more they realize how little they know. They're always making new discoveries about language, including discoveries about their own mother tongues.

To use an analogy, you may think you know your own mother. But what if one day you come across a chest hidden in the attic filled with diaries your mother wrote when she was a teenager? It turned out your mother is a bit of a mystery. Convinced you knew everything about her, you discovered she's not who you thought she was.

Often, when you think you know people or things intimately—like the language you speak or the family members that you see every day—they end up surprising and perplexing you.

Along the same vein, you may think that you know your native tongue. But have you ever experienced words failing you? Think about that time you had a brilliant idea and couldn't wait to tell everyone about it. When you found an audience of friends to talk to, you may have struggled to articulate your marvelous idea. Your friends came with their own preconceptions. No one heard your idea one way, or for that matter, the way you intended it to be heard.

Or perhaps you've had the experience sitting in the audience of an incredible dance performance, hearing a symphony that blew your mind, or gazing at a clear night sky full of stars. Sometimes it's neither you nor your audience's fault that no words can capture what you saw, heard, or felt. Words alone can be futile. When you feel something powerfully, language often struggles to contain your sense of awe.

For over ten years, I have worked professionally as a linguist and translator. My day-to-day work is steeped in language. I am always, perhaps ironically, struggling with it. I speak Chinese and English fluently, but at least a thousand times I've said to myself, "My Chinese (or English) is not good enough."

Where do those feelings of inadequacy come from? It can't be that I'm incompetent. Even the most competent translators and interpreters share my frustrations. To work across two languages makes it easier to realize the limitations of words.

Linguists are not the only ones who, immersed in words, find them limited.

Take William Shakespeare. Widely regarded as one of the greatest writers in the English language, his poems and plays celebrate language. But his characters often question the meaning of words and if words are entirely adequate to convey feeling and experience. In Shakespeare's play *Hamlet*, the prince is mourning the death of his father. He struggles to find meaning not only within the world but within words. When his girlfriend's father—a man with no loss for words—approaches Hamlet when he's reading a book, he asks him: "What do you read, my lord?" Hamlet responds: "Words, words, words." As much as Hamlet loves words—evidenced in his intricate soliloquies—when the prince wanders despondently around the castle, words, he soon realizes, can be trivial, trite, and meaningless. They act as weak containers for his inner life, which overflows with ineffable grief.[39]

Or take Lily Briscoe from Virginia Woolf's *To the Lighthouse*. Lily is a painter, who struggles to make sense of both the world and her inner life. Language doesn't always suffice. "And to those words, what meaning attached, after all?" she says.[40] Gustav Flaubert's character Rodolph Boulanger in *Madame Bovary* also struggles with words. To him, words can hardly hold a candle to his love interest, Emma Bovary. "Human speech is like a cracked tin kettle," he says, "on which we hammer out our tunes to make bears dance when we long to move the stars."[41]

Did Shakespeare, Woolf, and Flaubert consider language inadequate? Masters of their craft, they too longed "to move the stars" but sometimes felt that they were hammering out tunes on a cracked kettle. Most writers write draft after draft, struggling with syntax and sentences. The quote, "there is no such thing as good writing, only good rewriting," has been attributed to so many writers—from Robert Graves to Roald Dahl—that it's clear that writing is not a single activity, but a range of processes that include planning, drafting, revising, editing and rewriting.[42]

Words can beguile, disappoint, and evade any one of us. The magical thing about language is that it seems to be operating under a fixed set of structures and rules, and yet, it is always bending those rules. In his response to the rule "never end the sentence with a preposition," Winston Churchill said: "From now on, ending a sentence with a preposition is something up with which I will not put."[43] He satirized pedantic adherence to this rule.

Even more mysterious is that no one knows who invented the rules. That's why linguists say that language is arbitrary. It's based on random choices rather than reason. You don't learn to speak your mother tongue by studying the system that governs it. You learn basic vocabulary; then, you're able to communicate.

If you study a language long enough, you may get a sense that you've mastered its rules. But there's no way that anyone can truly master a language. There's always a sense of incompleteness, or something unrecognizable, living within the words we speak. Maggie Stiefvater writes in the young adult novel *The Raven King*, "It wasn't that Henry was less of himself in English. He was less of himself out loud. His native language was thought."[44] The language you call your mother tongue, despite its cosy familiarity, can at times stir up an unsettling feeling of homelessness—or a sense that its words are somehow insufficient to convey emotion and meaning. You may even wonder at times if your mother tongue is indeed your own.

In a way, we're all orphans of language and foster children to our mother tongues. Given that we're all constantly trying to make sense of our lives through language, it might be hard to accept that the language we speak doesn't belong to us. Just as children usually live in their mother's home, we all live in language. We depend on it for survival. Try to name one thing you've done successfully without any reference to or use of language. I bet you can—but I bet there aren't many. Even when you sleep, you use language to dream. Right now, you're creating meanings from the words on this page. You're arriving at your own understanding based on how you relate to the text, on how it makes you feel.

Everyone has her own experience with language. You learn how to speak in your own way from the people and environment that you're most familiar with. The meanings of words can be fickle, but language itself is fluid and dynamic. It changes as it moves through the minds and mouths of individuals. Its meaning shifts depending on the context. How often have you felt that someone's words were open to more than one interpretation? Chances are, even when meanings appear relatively fixed and stable, words evoke multiple meanings and associations.

Have you ever read a book at two different stages of your life? You may have found the book has two meanings. One relates to your younger self, and another makes sense to your older self.

That's why it helps to look at the meanings of words with an open mind. It is all too easy to arrive at meaning, (or judgement), based solely on the interpretations we're used to. We might think, unconsciously, that the meanings we've created are the only window to the world we live in. Every day, we take meaning for granted, no matter what language we speak. We all find justification for our interpretations.

For example, someone who has been exposed to a terrorist attack might think the whole world is a dangerous place. A child who has never been praised by a parent or teacher might think she is never good enough for anyone. A wife whose husband has left her may think she is not worthy of love. A patient who believes that he is dying may not believe his doctor's optimistic message about his recovery. There's truth to the saying, "We don't see things as they are, we see them as we are."

Of course, language is not the only medium we use to create and convey meaning. Painters like Paul Klee or Wassily Kandinsky used signs, symbols and colors. Vocalists like Aretha Franklin used pitch and tone. Dancers like Martha Graham and Merce Cunningham communicated through gesture and movement. But does any painter own the color blue, any singer the B minor tone, or any dancer the gesture of a hand lifting?

Linguistic taboos: What makes bad words bad?

If we don't own the words we speak, nor create the meanings of them, then who does? The culture? Or society? After all, we share our meanings and associations attached to certain words within a particular cultural group. How are these meanings produced? How do they make an impact on us? To answer these questions, let's start with "bad" words we'd rather not speak or hear.

Can you think of any words that you wouldn't say in public? Or maybe there

66

are phrases that you'd be embarrassed to say to your grandmother? Each culture has its own restrictions around what is socially acceptable to say aloud. They're called linguistic taboos. To avoid using them, people often rely on euphemisms, or mild, or indirect words and phrases to stand in for words that may sound too harsh, rude or unacceptable to say aloud. In nearly every language, you can find dozens of expressions to mean "to die." "Kick the bucket," "passed away" and "bit the dust" are but a few. If you're ever been fired from a job, you have a whole gamut of phrases to choose from when you want to break the news: "I was let go," "I'm between jobs," or "I've taken an early retirement."

Many colloquial expressions of surprise and fear in English are euphemisms for the names of religious figures. When used without disguise, they might be taken as profane or sacrilegious. Expressions like "Jeez," "Jeepers Creepers," and "Gee Whiz" are all euphemisms for "Jesus Christ." Words like "Golly" and "Gosh" have been in circulation so long that most people have forgotten that they were originally euphemisms for "God."

Even if you're not religious, there are probably more than a few words you feel uncomfortable saying. In nearly every society, the naming of certain body parts has become taboo. Naming those parts in public may not be breaking the law, but it can mean breaking a social construct or contract. In Chinese culture, words like rape and masturbation are traditionally considered taboo. (Although, for the younger generations, they are not considered as taboos necessarily).

A lot of linguistic taboos revolve around sex, a phenomenon that fascinated Sigmund Freud. Freud thought that sexual repression lies behind many of our everyday motivations, emotions, and behaviors. Buried deeply within the unconscious, the shame many people feel around sex can, according Freud, lead to neuroses—or worse—crime. It makes perfect sense that many of us feel embarrassed or uncomfortable when we hear words that hint at sexuality. If any truth lies behind Freud's theories, the social restrictions that societies have put around sexuality have only added to its collection of linguistic taboos.

Of course, linguistic taboos are not in themselves "bad." Alone, taboos are neither moral nor immoral. But taboos can trigger a range of emotions, some of which might feel "bad" to some people. Linguistic taboos are often charged with intense emotions, personal stories, and cultural interpretations.

Take the word "rape." Many people feel uncomfortable saying the word, and each culture has built its own meanings and associations around rape. When we think of the word rape, it often leads us to think of other emotionally-charged words such as victim, violence, and impurity. The word rape on its own causes neither insult nor injury. But our individual and cultural associations with rape often generate fear, which is one of our most primal emotions. Psychologically, fear is connected to states of insecurity and uncertainty. Stephen King depicted men in prison fearing rape in his novella *Rita Hayworth and Shawshank Redemption*.[45] Rape itself is frightening, but the fear of it also reflects the insecurity and uncertainty of prison life. The humiliation of being a victim of rape can be equally as terrifying.

Is it possible to imagine rape outside of our own social, cultural, and individual constructs? The American poet and visual artist Vanessa Place works as a criminal defence lawyer. She represents convicted sex offenders on appeal. In her 2010 book *The Guilt Project: Rape, Morality and Law*, she argues that rape is more of a social and moral crime than a legal one.[46] She asks a difficult question, "*What do the ways we punish and demonize sex offenders say about us as a culture?* In her 2019 book *You Had to Be There*, Place weaves together 130-plus pages of jokes about rape, many of which she gathered from the dark corners of the internet.[47] Shining a spotlight on the taboo of rape, the jokes—whether they lead to laughter or rage—cause discomfort for most readers. In a 2017 interview with *Artforum*, the artist says that many of us live with the "fantasy of possible purity." The jokes she's collected, ask us to confront the violence that has always existed, a violence we are complicit in. [48]

In Chinese film and television, popular melodramas of ancient palace life often tell the story of a concubine who dreams of the Emperor laying eyes on her. She desires any physical contact with him and envies the woman that the Emperor "favors." In that context, when the Emperor forces himself on a woman, he doesn't "rape" her. He "favors" her. The language used to refer to the act of sexual coercion alters the cultural and emotional associations we have with it. In modern societies, rape is a crime. In palace life in ancient China, it was legitimized and normalized.

Members of a group usually share collective interpretations of words. A study conducted by professors of psychology at The University of California and Yonsei University reveals that Koreans and Americans have differing interpretations of the word "happiness." Koreans tend to associate "happiness" with social terms that indicate relationship, like "family." Americans most commonly associate the word "happiness" with the word "smile."[49]

Sometimes the meanings of words become institutionalized. Members of a group take them for granted and lose the ability to look at them with a critical eye. Academic language, for example, can often be impenetrable to anyone outside an academic institution. Academic writing that focuses on examining and overcoming social inequality often does so in a language that ironically perpetuates inequality. Researchers use terms like "intersectionality" and "positionality" with the intent of examining systems of discrimination or disadvantage. But few people, let alone those without access to higher education, understand those terms.

Or consider how language is regulated. Taboos are rarely acknowledged openly in any culture. But like the human actions they allude to, taboos are infused with social or cultural meanings. They are based upon what sociologists Martyn Hammersley and Paul Atkinson refer to as "intentions, motives, beliefs, rules, discourse, and values." [50]

But what do Hammersley and Atkinson mean by "discourse?" It's an institutional-sounding word, isn't it? But don't let that put you off just yet. It holds some clues to how our minds work.

Discourse: How are words acting upon us?

What comes to mind when you hear the word "discourse?"

The word sounds a lot like "discussion," "discuss," or "discursive." You can think of discourse as written or spoken communication. Academics use the word a lot, but they didn't invent it. It had its origin from Latin, in which the prefix dis- means "away" and the root word *currere* means "to run."[51]

Think of having a good conversation with friends. Doesn't it often "run about" from topic to topic? Can't it digress, drift off on tangents, and meander back again?

For linguists, the topic of good conversation is often conversation itself. Linguists study conversation. They study language usage, the shape that language takes in conversations. By conversation, I don't necessarily mean dialog. "Conversation" might refer to language usage in a book, a document, a newspaper, or a speech. Think of it as any form of communication when there is a potential audience.

Linguists enjoy asking questions like: *How is language functioning in this text? Why does it use "we" most of the time and shift to the use of "they" suddenly? What are the assumptions behind that? How does it make the audience feel?*

Zellig Harris first described this as "discourse analysis."[52] Again, don't let that fancy term make you think that only specialists can study language. You too can study the connection between sentences—or analyse discourse. If you pay attention to conversations, to the patterns of words and sentences, and the connectedness between sentences and paragraphs, you'll likely see beyond what David Block calls the "nuts and bolts"of language. Grammar is not the only thing that determines how we use language.

Norman Fairclough, a professor of linguistics at The University of Lancaster, suggests that speech, or discourse, is fundamentally a social practice.[53] The way we speak creates a sense of unity both psychologically and culturally. It gives people within a group a sense of shared meaning. Discourse shapes how people in a group perceive, experience, and articulate the world. For example, the media has its own way of speaking, its own discourse. The ways that television programs represent other cultures influence how people perceive those cultures.

When a few of my American friends visited China for the first time, they told me that they were surprised at what they found there. They were surprised to see that China is advancing technologically, that its citizens talk about politics and its people have progressive ideas. Americans with no first-hand experience of China will often only have seen media depictions. Their views have been shaped by media discourse, which is true in any country. American television doesn't necessarily tell its viewers outright that China is a backward-thinking, conservative country where people lack any freedom of speech. Instead, the media uses language in a way that implies that perspective. That's how discourse works. Television speaks to its viewers in ways that the viewers are not fully aware of, and that shapes public opinion.

The way people of a culture speak also produces how and what they know. Knowledge, like language, can be produced, institutionalized and ingrained in our social customs. The books you read in school were likely filled with different facts than the schoolbooks of your father or grandfather. In Japanese schools in 2020, students learn different history lessons than their grandfathers did. In particular, the historical perspective of Japan's relationship with China has changed over time. It isn't that history itself has changed; the discourse about it has changed.

Unlike the young Victor of Aveyron, we depend on other human beings for our identity, language, and survival. Human beings are social animals. Through relationships, we learn to speak, read, and create. Whenever we want to make something, like a house or a meal, we need to cooperate with other humans to see it through. Karl Marx suggests that in order to produce things, human beings must enter into relationships with others.[54] When we belong within a group, we usually exhibit similar speech patterns and behaviors.

Some cultures emphasize individuality. But the need to belong with a group is prevalent and primal. Even teenagers who rebel against the status quo are often embarrassed if they're asked to dress differently than their rebellious peers. In Western culture, innovation is encouraged. But adults are often reluctant to express new ideas if they differ too much from those of their colleagues. If you've ever experienced culture shock, or even identity conflict, when you're in a foreign country, you know the feeling. Whether you have a lot in common with people in a foreign culture is irrelevant. On the surface, you stand out, and that can lead you to feel insecure and unsettled. That's why expats often hang out with other expats from their home country. If they were to meet the same people at home, they might not share the same level of affinity with them.

Like language and perception, the ways that we acquire knowledge—our cognition—is a social act. How we know things is grounded in relationships. We acquire knowledge through interaction. We inherit meanings, perspectives and assumptions from the cultures we live in. Often, we do this without noticing. Take the sentence: "Mary Curie is one of the most celebrated female scientists." If you know Marie Curie and her contributions to cancer research, you'll likely agree. But what about this statement? "Newton is one of the most influential male scientists." Does that sound odd to you? For most people, "male scientist" stands out as peculiar. But we are used to hearing "female" before the names of many occupations.

Why is that? Despite our cultural advances toward gender equality, many of us are still living within the echoes of an old system. For centuries, men dominated the economic sphere, and it was rare for women to have their own professions. A cultural bias still exists. That bias assumes that men are better suited to certain careers, particularly in the sciences. The traces of an old belief system surface in the ways we speak daily. We still use words like "policeman," "handyman" and "mailman" even though all those professions now include women.

Let's look at another example of discourse. We often use the terms "native" and "non-native speaker." Each illustrates whether or not someone was born into a particular language. At first glance, the two terms appear straightforward and not particularly controversial. But if you dig further, you might notice that a dichotomy exists between "native" and "non-native" that may be discriminatory in certain situations. Are those categories—native and non-native—fixed, mutually exclusive and non-negotiable? If a woman were born in China but raised in the United States, would she be a non-native English speaker? Underpinning the discourse of "native" and "non-native" are fixed ideas about who we are.

When language schools recruit English teachers, they often look for "native speakers." But are native and non-native English speakers all that different? Are they "two different species," to borrow the term coined by Hungarian linguist Péter Medgyes?[55] Several studies have shown pedagogical advantages of non-native teachers. In an interview I had with students in the university where I work, students said that they appreciate the cross-cultural perspectives and experiences brought by native teachers, but they also benefit from the ways that non-native teachers understand their challenges.

Perhaps the problem lies less in how we view native and non-native speakers and more in how language is inherently full of dichotomies and limitations. Right and wrong, true and false, justice and injustice. When we hear words like "Christian" and "Buddhist," for example, we think of two separate categories, two discrete religious affiliations. Of course, Christianity and Buddhism have different stories, traditions and teachers. But they share many of the same core values of compassion and generosity.

We are social animals. We thrive in the sense of belonging that comes with identifying with one group. But when we identify too stringently with one affiliation, we run the risk of pigeonholing ourselves and others in a way that betrays our own freedom.

Inner reality: Do you really own your thoughts?

As I write this, a highly contagious respiratory illness caused by a novel coronavirus (2019-nCoV) has caused a global pandemic. It's upturned global infrastructures and has forced people to stay home. First detected in Wuhan City, Hubei Province, China, the virus is believed to have originated in the local wet market that sells animals for human consumption. Some media outlets have gone so far to call it the "Wuhan virus." In China, other news outlets have been broadcasting that an American military athlete, Maatje Benassi, brought the virus to China.

Highly contagious, the coronavirus is hard to trace. Some people who get it show no symptoms. For those who do, they often feel like they're experiencing the seasonal flu, which complicates diagnoses. Initial figures from China and Italy suggested that the death rate from the virus is between 5–15 percent, similar to that of the 1918 Spanish flu pandemic. Other countries report a death rate of 0.4% or lower. How deadly is this virus? It's still far from clear.

As a linguist, what I find interesting about this pandemic are the many interpretations of the virus. There are many theories around its origins and its implications for humanity. Undoubtedly, the health crisis has caused a great deal of uncertainty on many fronts: economically, personally, and politically. When faced with crises, people tend to reach out for explanations. They often look to answers that confirm their worldview. How you experience a crisis reflects how you frame it and interpret it. Each of us has accumulated our own facts and feelings about infectious diseases and what they mean for our societies, our bodies, and ourselves.

Our capacity for language is coded in the neural networks in our brains. But is an individual's response to a crisis based in biology? Are some individuals born with predispositions for optimism or pessimism? Is how we interpret the world inherited from our ancestors and encoded in our genes?

As early as infanthood, you began exploring your environment. You made sense of the world based on your earliest experiences. You were surprisingly sophisticated at distinguishing familiar sounds from unfamiliar ones. You responded to your mother's voice in ways you didn't to a stranger's. You identified your father's voice as distinct from the sounds of the vacuum cleaner, the fridge, and the doorbell. The way you interpreted sounds was unique to you. As you grew up, you continued to respond to stimuli in the environment in ways that made the most sense for you. Your early responses influenced the ways you constructed meaning.

As you matured, you began to attach greater significance to certain events and experiences. You felt joy when you heard the sound of your mother laughing. You felt fear when you heard the neighbour's dog barking. You felt anticipation when the doorbell rang. Those experiences and your interpretations of them shaped how you went on to process new stimuli in the environment. When you heard laughter that was not your mother's, you may not have felt the same joy. When you heard a doorbell on the television, it likely stimulated feelings of anticipation of someone entering the house.

All the events that have made an impact on you—whether felt within the family, seen on television, or read in books—constitute a complex network of inner values and associations. That network shapes how you see the world. It weaves the fabric of your inner life. It maintains your sense of self, your narrative, and your worldview. And yet, you are unaware of it happening. Responses to your environment often feel instinctual. You might even find yourself struggling with two conflicting interpretations of one experience, torn between two instinctual responses.

You may be familiar with the cartoon television image of an angel and devil resting on a person's left and right shoulders. One represents your conscience, the other your temptation. You may not literally see two figures on each of your shoulders, but have you ever heard two inner voices, each giving you contradictory advice? One says, "Don't eat that chocolate!" or "A moment on the lips is a lifetime on the hips!" Another cajoles you in the opposite direction: "One last piece won't kill you!" When at work, you may have heard a strict voice demand: "You have to finish this today! People are counting on you!" The other contested: "Why not take some time for yourself?" Often when people find themselves in an uncertain romantic relationship, their two inner voices debate furiously. One argues: "Leave this person. She makes you feel that you're unworthy of love!" The other protests: "But where would you be without her?"

What is it about the mind that leads to two voices competing for our attention? What makes our inner lives so divided? Often those two voices go head to head when we're making a decision that might change the course of our lives. Our conflicting characters often have it out with each other until one gives into the other. Who's right and who's wrong? What is good and what is bad? Which voice is heroic and which villainous? Which is brave and which cowardly?

Which voice is you? The real you?

What if I said, "Neither!" Panksepp tells us that one voice comes from the lower brain—which drives instinctual, primary desires, and emotions—and the other from the higher brain, which drives cognitive thinking and is shaped by education. One voice wants you to avoid pain. The other wants you to regulate your primary emotions through higher levels of cognition. One voice is shared by animals. If you've ever lived with a dog, you might appreciate how they both avoid pain and nurture the connections with the people they live with. But unlike humans, dogs have little ability for higher levels of cognitive thinking.

Panskepp argues that the struggle between our two voices arises because of the way the human brain operates. Unlike a wild animal, an adult human regulates his primary emotions through higher levels of cognition. When confronted with a box of cookies, the higher brain functions that regulate emotion and inspire self-control too often succumb to the desire to avoid the pain of hunger and experience the pleasure of chocolate melting across your tongue. Emotions often override thoughts.

If your lower brain functioning trumps your higher brain functioning, what can you do about it? Are you doomed to live as a slave to your instincts? Or is it possible to prevent them from driving your day-to-day behavior? Believe it or not, by applying the practical insights of neuroscience through the use of language, you can make peace between those pestering voices waging a war inside of you. When you develop a clearer understanding of your emotions, and how language shapes your emotional experience, you can train your brain to reprogram how it responds to feelings, thoughts and events. You'll learn to embrace healthier feelings, thoughts, and actions. You'll learn this in the next chapter.

In Summary

Humans develop speech both by natural inclinations and through interactions within a language-rich environment. The way we speak and the words we use reflect the impact of the geography, culture, and milieu we live within. Giving this, can we claim that the words we speak are our own?

In this chapter, I presented three primary arguments.

1. We don't own our words.
    - We, including the most sophisticated writers, all struggle with words.
    - Language doesn't always suffice. There's a limitation about words.
    - Meanings of words are open to interpretations. Language is fluid and dynamic.
    - Our mother tongue can stir up an unsettling feeling of homelessness.

2. Words act upon us.
    - Taboos are not bad in themselves. They are bad because of the social and cultural meanings that a culture attaches to it.

- We inherit meanings and assumptions from the culture we live in.
- The way people of a culture speaks produces how and what they know.
- Discourse—language in use—is fundamentally a social practice. It shapes how people in a group perceive, experience, and articulate the world.

3. We don't own our thoughts.
   - We make sense of the world based on our earliest experiences. All the events that have impacted us constitute a complex network of inner values and associations. They form the basis of how we think and live.
   - According to neuroscience, our lower brain drives thoughts connected with instinctual, primary desires, and emotions. In contrast, the upper brain drives higher cognitive thinking that regulates primary emotions.
   - Through the use of language, you can train your brain to reprogram how it responds to feelings, thoughts, and events, bringing out healthier feelings, thoughts, and actions.

Chapter 5: Language Shapes Your Emotional Experience

"There's no mode of action, no form of emotion, that we do not share with the lower animals. It is only by language that we rise above them."

Oscar Wilde[56]

"We often use strong language not to express a powerful emotion but to evoke it in us."

Eric Hoffer[57]

"Each of you possesses the most powerful, dangerous and subversive trait that natural selection has ever devised. It's a piece of neural audio technology for rewriting other people's mind. I'm talking about language."

Mark Pagel[58]

Words make us laugh. They make us weep. They seize us in uncontrollable rage. They can also calm us into angel-like tranquillity. Language does not only help us communicate our feelings. It evokes them.

Amongst the long list of English words that arouse strong emotions[59], "pervert" is certainly one of them. If you hear the word "pervert," without a doubt, it will make you feel unpleasant. It's a provocative expression that we'd all prefer no one throws our way.

But language that triggers us doesn't have to be in the form of name-calling. Many words trigger either positive or negative emotions—or both, depending on the context. Hearing words like "divorce," "affair" or "romance" amidst a painful separation might lead one person to feel disgust, anger or envy. To someone falling in love, "romance" is the sweetest thing.

The magic of language lies less in the way it evokes emotions in real life and more in the way it evokes them in the imagination. Language gives wings to our imaginations. It enables us to invent characters whose joy and sorrow we can feel. Language helps us empathize with someone we've never met or who doesn't even exist.

Have you ever read a novel that you simply couldn't put down? You may have cried when the main character was suffering or felt lifted up when she overcame a difficult situation. Sometimes the emotions you have when you're reading can haunt you long after you've put the book down.

Or perhaps you've watched a film about star-crossed lovers? You didn't need to experience their feelings first-hand to feel sympathy for them. You knew they were only actors and that their emotions were staged. But you suspended your disbelief. You got caught up in the story, just as if it were real, just as if it were happening to you. Even if a story is not real, your tears are. Your brain can't tell the difference between what is real and what is imagined.[60]

Have you ever cried when sharing a story to a friend about your own life? Maybe you talked about the pain of losing someone. It may have been a breakup, divorce, or death in the family. Even if you'd gotten over it, when you talked to someone about the loss, you teared up. Articulating something painful through language can evoke the deep-seated pain that is still alive within you.

But the role of language goes well beyond the triggering of emotions. If words trigger emotions, then they also trigger neural changes in the brain. Our brain, according to Panksepp, is driven primarily by emotional experiences.[61] Emotions dictate our thoughts and behavior. But language plays a more profound role in the way we perceive and experience emotion than we'd assumed. Professor Cathy Price, a clinical psycholinguist at UCL Wellcome Trust Centre for Neuroimaging, writes that when we use language, we use "most of our brain." Language integrates "all of our sensory resources, all the different types of memory that we can have and then coordinates how we respond." Indeed, "everything we do is monitored by language."[62]

Understanding the role language plays in our emotional lives as well as our everyday perceptions and thoughts has important implications for how we take care of ourselves—how we regulate our emotions and foster healthier thoughts, feelings, and actions. All of that is critical for our overall well-being.

Experiencing emotions in a foreign language

When I was teaching online recently, I overheard a student say: "Shit!" He had made a mistake when typing in the chat box and had forgotten to mute himself. Hearing a student swear does not surprise me. I used to hear Chinese students swear in English on campus now and again. But I have yet to hear a Chinese student swear in Chinese.

I sympathize with that student who blurted out a four-letter word in my class. I, too, have used English words to express disgust or disbelief. When I hear an adult using abusive language to a child, I say: "Goddammit!" When I receive a text message at midnight asking me to check my email, I might think to myself: "Jesus!" I feel a release of negative feelings I've been holding when I swear in English, my second language. But unlike the occasions when I swear in Chinese, I never feel I am being rude when I swear in English. Swearing in a language that is not my mother tongue doesn't feel uncivilized to me. Interesting, no? Even more interesting is that hearing a swear word in another language feels less offensive.

 An English friend of mine said that one of his colleagues had an umbrella emblazoned with the message: *"Merde, il pleut."* Had the umbrella said, "Shit, it's raining," he might have hesitated to walk around London with it. In Douglas Adams's *The Hitchhiker's Guide to the Galaxy*, the most terrible profanity, the word that horrifies people across the galaxy, is "Belgium."[63] Adams illustrates a telling point about our attitudes toward language. We tolerate swear words from a foreign culture, in a foreign language. Had Adams replaced "Belgium" with "America" and his characters were horrified every time they heard the word "America," he would have no doubt offended many of his American readers.

Speaking in a foreign language can mitigate the intensity of our feelings.[64] English swear words are less triggering to non-native speakers than they are to native speakers. Non-native English speakers are less likely to have personal associations with English profanities. They are less likely to take them to heart. They're less likely to have been shouted at or demeaned by an English swear word. Nelson Mandela said: "If you talk to a man in a language he understands, that goes to his head. If you talk to him in his language, that goes to his heart."[65]

When I teach, I sometimes prefer to speak Chinese even in a class of English majors, where the mainstream opinion advocates the pure use of the English language or the immersion environment of the English language. I do that not only because it helps me to explain difficult concepts to my Chinese students. It also helps me establish rapport with them when I tell a story or we chat informally at the beginning of the class. Most of my students have good English listening skills. But when I speak Chinese to them, I feel closer to them, as if we were speaking mind-to-mind and heart-to-heart. Communicating in our shared native tongue enables me to feel like I am a friend to them. It helps me feel more amiable and approachable.

When I am explaining to my students areas where they have done poorly, how they could improve their attitude or why they could perform better, I use English. In that way, feedback feels less personal, and it's less likely that they will harbor harsh feelings after hearing it.

Language is your telescope

Emotions are abstractions. Surprised? It's true that when you feel something strongly, you feel concrete sensations in your body. But the words you use to describe what you're feeling—whether "love," "fear," or "excitement"—are abstract nouns. They exist as a thought or idea but do not have a concrete physical existence.

Imagine you're about to give a speech in front of a large audience. You might feel heat rising to your face and your heart beating faster than normal. As your adrenal glands flood the body with stress hormones, your muscles may tense up. Your blood pressure might rise, and your breath may quicken. You might call what you are experiencing "nervousness," "fear," or "excitement."

Or, imagine you're riding a train. You see a teenager behaving poorly to an elderly woman. Chances are your body will exhibit similar responses as it does when you're afraid. But you might name your response differently. You feel "anger" instead of "fear."

Why do we have different words for similar physiological reactions?

Before you label what you're feeling as "fear," "excitement" or "anger," you experience a vague sense of intense, generally negative, feelings. In the case of "excitement," you likely experience a vague sense of intense, generally positive, feelings. Those vague feelings—whether positive or negative—are called affect, a term that refers to a neurophysiological state characterized by pleasure or displeasure, high arousal or low arousal.[66]

Humans are full of affect. We have a whole galaxy of subtle or strong and simple or complex feelings in us. You are conscious of many of those feelings without having access to language, just as you are conscious of the stars without having access to a telescope. But language acts like a telescope that brings those vague feelings into focus. It enables you to perceive the distinct qualities of your feelings, make sense of their presence in your life and label them, which helps you to preserve their place in your personal narrative.

Ancient Greek astronomers named groups of stars, or constellations, after the shapes the patterns of stars formed. The constellation Scorpio looks like a scorpion. Cygnus looks like a swan. But those names also preserved Ancient Greek folklore and mythology. The constellation of Orion refers to the son of the Ancient Greek sea god, Poseidon, a great hunter. Ancient Egyptians, who looked up at the same pattern of stars, called it not Orion but Osiris, who was in Ancient Egyptian culture the deity of life and death.

All of us may have similar structures to our emotional brains and share similar affect. But how we label our feelings depends on the language we speak, the culture we live in and the stories we live by. People all over the world experience a pleasant feeling when walking in the woods. But only in Dutch can you call that feeling *uitwaaien*. You've likely felt feelings of courage throughout your life, but unless you're Finnish, you won't view those feelings as *sisu*, a Finnish word that means extraordinary determination in the face of adversity. In Portuguese, if you feel melancholic longing or wistful nostalgia for something far away, you're experiencing *saudade*.

If you've been to Portugal, you know that *saudade* lives and breathes in the streets of Porto and Lisbon. A whole tradition of music in Portugal, *fado*, speaks to this melancholic, mournful quality of missing someone or something. And if there's one word that characterizes Finnish culture, it's *sisu*; Finns ascribe an almost mystical quality to *sisu*.

We can't name a feeling if we have neither the language nor the upbringing to perceive it. The ancient astronomer Ptolemy named 48 constellations. Those constellations have formed the basis of our modern understanding of our galaxy. But without a telescope, much of the Southern Hemisphere remained invisible to Ptolemy. Astronomers have now recognized 88 constellations. But there are still billions of stars, many of which remain invisible—hence, nameless—to us, even with all our advancements in technology.

Words to name emotions, just like words to name stars and constellations, are all constructs. No star is born with the name "Sirius." No constellation comes together on its own, let alone under names like "Pegasus" or "Little Bear." And just as there is a limit to our identification of the stars in the night sky, there's a limit to the number of feelings we can perceive.

Have you ever found it difficult to express in words what you feel? Or have you ever experienced complicated ambiguous feelings that you find difficult to categorize under a single word like "joy" or "sadness"? Those limitations explain the sense of inadequacy many of us feel about language. In Jeffrey Eugenides' novel *Middlesex*, the narrator Cal explains it this way:

"Emotions, in my experience, aren't covered by single words. I don't believe in "sadness," "joy" or "regret." Maybe the best example proof that language is patriarchal is that it oversimplifies feelings. I'd like to have at my disposal complicated hybrid emotions, Germanic train-car constructions like say, "the happiness that attends to disaster"... I'd like to have a word for "the sadness inspired by failing restaurants" as well as for "the excitement of getting a room with a minibar." I've never had the right words to describe my life, and now that I've entered my story, I need them more than ever."[67]

Despite the inadequacy of single words to articulate Cal's emotions, the narrator still uses language to describe what he calls "complicated hybrid feelings". "The sadness inspired by failing restaurants" is evocative. "The excitement of getting a room with a minibar" is familiar to anyone who's rented a hotel room for the night. But only by identifying that peculiar and complex feeling in language can Cal, or anyone, appreciate it fully.

By naming emotions, whether in single words or in complicated phrases, you shape the perception and experience of your own feelings. When you say: "I feel nervous" instead of "I feel a vague sense of generally negative feelings," you are narrating your emotional life, giving it a character and form. If you were to say: "I feel the sadness inspired by failing restaurants" when you see the sushi shop on the corner going out of business, it gives tone, quality and particularity to your experience.

Infants and animals do not have access to language. They cannot name their emotions; although, they do have core affect. Once children acquire language, they can transform those vague sensations of pleasure and displeasure, high arousal and low arousal, into discrete and specific types of emotions.[68] They learn to categorize sensations by referring to the concept of "fear" and "anger." While your breath may quicken and your heart rate might go up when you experience both fear and anger, you've learned through the use of language to distinguish between the two emotions.

The words you use to describe specific emotions—like "fear" and "anger"—help you make sense of your response to either internal or external stimuli.

Your physiological reactions in your body happen before your cerebral cortex begins to make sense of what is happening. Your body responds before your mind identifies the experience of all those intense sensations as "anger" or "fear."

Developmental and cognitive scientists have observed that language is what gives form and structure to abstract concepts.[69] Language enables us to feel, see and understand the world in a way that is impossible for animals. The language we use to describe emotions is an example of how we use words to give shape to abstract concepts.

Take the word "love." Love is one of the most powerful yet mysterious abstractions that humans have a name for. The magazine *Coup de Main*, when interviewing musician Mark Hoppus, asked him what he felt was the strongest human emotion. Hoppus said what many people feel: "The strongest human emotion is probably love. I think it's universal. I think that across language and country and time and everything else, probably love."[70]

Although love might express itself in various ways across cultures, all languages have a word for "love."

You may have heard the expression "love conquers all" from the Roman poet Virgil's *Eclogues*, written in 38 BCE. The original is in Latin: "*Omina vincit amor et nos sedamus amori.*" In English, that means: "Love conquers all; let us too, yield to love!"[71]

Some of the most quoted passages from *The Bible* come from 1 Corinthians 13. The passage begins: "If I speak in the tongues of men and angels, but I have not love, I am only a resounding gong or clang or cymbal…if I have a faith that can move mountains, but I have not love, I am nothing." Knowledge passes away, languages pass away, but "Love never fails." The passage ends: "And now these three remain: faith, hope and love. But the greatest of these is love."[72]

Martin Luther King, Jr. said, "Love is the only force capable of transforming an enemy into a friend."[73] For Helen Keller, "Love is like a beautiful flower which I may not touch, but whose fragrance makes the garden a place of delight just the same."[74] For Leo Buscaglia, "Love is always bestowed as a gift—freely, willingly and without expectation. We don't love to be loved; we love to love."[75] For Lao Tzu, "Love is all passions the strongest, for it attaches simultaneously the head, the heart and the senses." [76]

What is love to you? You might feel as Martin Luther King, Helen Keller, or Lao Tzu does. Their words might describe perfectly how you feel when you love. Or you may be unclear if what you experience is love to begin with. Love has no singular, concrete form in any given culture. We can describe concrete examples of what we consider to be love, but the concept of love exists primarily in language.

Do emotions feel the same across cultures?

If words like "love," "hate," "envy," and "pride" are constructs or concepts in language, it makes sense to say emotions, like languages, have been shaped by culture.[77] Just as Chinese and English language have different words for "laugh," each culture has its own words to describe specific feelings. And as discussed, many words and expressions across cultures cannot be readily translated into other languages. No words in another language can accurately reflect all the shades and subtle nuances of particular words.

Take the word *toska* (pronounced tahs-kah) in Russian. What does that mean in English? According to a 2018 article in *The Guardian, toska* is one of the "10 best words in the world (that don't translate into English)."[78] Like the Portuguese word *saudade, toska* commonly translates as yearning or ennui. But since no English words do it complete justice, it's hard to grasp the subtleties of what *toska* means to Russians. Andrew Roth, *The Guardian's* correspondent in Moscow describes *toska* as "spiritual anguish, a deep pining, perhaps the product of nostalgia or love-sickness." It "is depression plus longing, an unbearable feeling that you need to escape but lack the hope or energy to do so."[79] You might need to read a novel by Dostoyevsky to get at the heart of it.

Japanese like to say *shoganai* to describe a situation that is out of their control. It might be a small situation, like forgetting your umbrella when it rains. Or it might be a serious situation, like an earthquake. When you describe a situation as *shoganai*, you feel incapable of doing anything to influence the outcome, but you also accept that it is what it is. *"C'est la vie,"* the French might say. The word *shoganai* has its roots in the Zen Buddhist belief that natural suffering is a necessary part of life.[80]

What's more, Japanese small emotive particles "ne", "na", "naa," and "yo" (ね、な、なあ、よ), often used at the end of the sentence, usually contain a difficult-to-explain emotion or emphasis. The nuances they carry could be different when used in a different context, and there is no single word or simple expressions in English (and in many cases, this is true in Chinese, too) that reflect and capture the meanings of those nuances.

In Chinese, a lot of four-word character expressions are difficult to translate. Many of them have an anecdote or story behind them. Or, they have been taken from a well-known source, like ancient poetry. Take 春风得意 *(chun feng de yi)* as an example. The characters 春风 *(Chun feng)* mean "spring breeze." The second two 得意 *(de yi)* mean "content and proud." You might find it strange to combine "spring breeze" and "content and proud" to express a feeling. But it comes from a line of poetry by Mengjiao in the Tang Dynasty: "Light-hearted in the spring breeze, my horse's hoofs run fast; In a single day I have seen all the flowers of Ch'ang-an."[81] In two lines, the poet describes how he feels after succeeding in the imperial exam. The phrase 春风得意 *(chun feng de yi)* describes a feeling of light-heartedness, contentment, fulfillment, and pride that accompanies success and achievement. There are no words in English that reflect the feeling accurately.

As with many expressions that have no English equivalents, *cheng fen de yi* speaks of something distinct in the culture that invented it. Traditional Chinese place emphasis on hard work, strong will to endure suffering (both of which are believed to be able to help harvest fine results), and respect for elders. Likewise, if you've ever spent a winter in Russia or have read Russian novels, you'll understand why there's no word in any other language that comes close to *toska*. Roth can even locate *toska* in the Russian landscape, in "an endless field of birch on the edge of St. Petersburg, in the dead of winter when the clouds never part."[82] The Russian writer Anton Chekhov even wrote a story called "Toska." In it, a lonely taxi driver grieves the death of his son, but he can only find consolation in his horse.

Words often embody the cultures that speak them. Even universally understood terms like "love" are shaped by the traditions of each culture. Words like "pride," "shame," "jealousy," or "trust" also take on distinct meanings in different cultures. In China, when a parent or a teacher says: "I feel proud of you," it's because the young person has achieved something remarkable. Traditionally, Chinese parents and teachers have strict standards and high expectations of young people. In English culture, a parent or teacher might say "I feel proud of you" when the child accomplishes something unremarkable but that has meaning for the child.

In a Western context, the word shame has derogatory connotations. When you do something shameful, it's usually held in contempt. If you were to cheat on an exam, you might feel ashamed. In Chinese culture, shame is an unpleasant emotion, but it can also be commendatory. In China, if you behave shamefully, you act outside of societal norms. It might be something trivial, like wearing the wrong clothes. Or it might be something significant, like cheating on a spouse. But if you feel shame, it means you can be forgiven.

Chinese culture interprets feeling shame as a sign that you recognize the wrongs you did and are willing to correct them. We have an expression in Chinese: "Not knowing the shame." It describes someone who is morally corrupt and beyond forgiveness. The concept of shame in Chinese culture affects how people react to acts of wrongdoing. In Western culture, feeling ashamed about an affair usually has little consequence for the outcome of a marriage. In Chinese culture, demonstrating that you feel ashamed about an affair might help you repair your broken relationship with your spouse.

How different people perceive emotion is relative to both the cultural context and the individual. Kristen Lindquist, a professor of psychology and neuroscience at the University of North Carolina, Chapel Hill, studies the nature of emotions. In one study, she discovered that Chinese and English speakers perceive facial expressions in markedly different ways. Two groups— one English and the other Chinese—were asked to match facial expressions with six different emotions: "happy," "surprised," "fearful," "disgusted," "angry" and "sad." English speakers were consistent in their responses. Amongst the Chinese, there was less consensus on which facial expression fell under which emotion. One person saw fear, another disgust and yet another anger.[83] It's worth noting that Chinese speakers were presented with translations of English words. That may explain the inconsistency.

The role of language in regulating our emotions

If language plays a role in how you perceive and experience emotion, it will also affect how you regulate your emotional life. Labeling feelings as soon as they arise can help mitigate phobias and stress.[84] Recently, researchers have observed in neuroimaging that the very act of labeling and categorizing a feeling influences the brain's processing of it. In one study, participants viewed pictures of negative facial expressions and were asked to label them from a fixed set of choices. The activity in their ventrolateral prefrontal cortex increased, and the activity in their amygdala decreased.[85] In other words, when you label an emotion, you engage the area of your brain responsible for cognitive control of your behavior. You turn down the dial in the area of the brain responsible for involuntary "fight or flight" reactions. In short, you regain control of your experience and become less emotionally reactive.

Another study presented participants with threatening images, which naturally led to them to experience negative feelings.[86] But those who labeled their feelings experienced fewer involuntary reactions. Another study observed that regions of the brain that are active when labeling a feeling overlap with those regions responsible for emotional regulation.[87] To put that in context, if you were to perceive something as threatening on the street—a dog growling and baring its teeth—you might have a range of involuntary reactions. Your muscles might tense up, and your heart rate might increase. Without emotional regulation, you might start panicking and feel you've lost control. If the dog reacts to your fear with more barking, you'll perceive an even greater threat, and that will only increase your fight or flight response. But if you label what you are feeling as "fear," you'll engage your prefrontal cortex, which enables you to act more rationally and exhibit greater overall cognitive control.

In social and political contexts, you see the results of unregulated emotional responses all the time. When a policeman suspects a man on the street is reaching for a gun, he may react unconsciously and involuntarily. Before he knows what is happening, he might fire his own gun, perceiving the man as a threat. He may later discover that the man he's shot had been reaching for a wallet and not a weapon. If that policeman had paused and labeled what he was experiencing as "fear," it might have given himself a chance to act with greater cognitive control.

Panksepp suggests that adults can regulate their primary emotions through higher levels of cognition, which is one activity that distinguishes the human brain from that of an animal.[88] When you experience desire, fear, anxiety or rage, you're experiencing them from your lower brain. When you use language to make sense of those desires, fears and anxieties, you're using the upper brain.

But the first step in regulating emotions is in getting in touch with them.

An action guide to get in touch with your emotions and find inner peace and happiness

Some people think that by ignoring or suppressing emotions, they are controlling them. But like living creatures, if you ignore or cage up your feelings, they don't disappear. Even exotic birds and grizzly bears in zoos need attention. To control wild animals, you have to first take care of them. To take charge of your emotions, you have to first attend to them.

When you get in touch with your emotions, when you stay in tune with how you truly feel, it's easier to regulate rage, fear or sadness. Surprised? There's evidence from neuroimaging studies that supports the benefits of becoming emotionally aware. Participants who could name the emotions they were experiencing, rather than simply perceive them as either generally positive or generally negative, demonstrated more activity in the region of anterior temporal lobe.[89] That's the brain region involved in the memory and knowledge we have of the world.

Your culture, like many cultures, may encourage you to put on a happy face even when you're feeling unhappy. Someone might ask: "Are you okay?" And you might say: "I'm just fine, thanks." You not only hide your true feelings, you hide your desires, needs and hopes—not to mention your true self—from the world.

But in that act of hiding, you might forget who you are. You might deny yourself permission to ask yourself what it is you truly desire, authentically need and genuinely hope for. If you keep neglecting your real feelings, they can accumulate and inflate. You might be tempted to bury them with food, alcohol, and drugs—or anything that numbs you from feeling what you truly feel. But eventually, those feelings burst, like a balloon filled with too much air.

Even if you don't have a tendency to turn to an addiction in an attempt to mute your feelings, you've probably experienced your own bubble bursting. Have you ever "blown up" at someone or said something that you later regretted? Perhaps you felt neglected by a partner or a friend, but you weren't honest about how that person's behavior affected how you felt. You buried your resentment. One day, you couldn't hold it in anymore. You lost control. You blew up. You burst your bubble.

If that's the case, don't be too hard on yourself. Emotional awareness is not something that our brains are hard-wired to do. If you want to be emotionally aware, you have to work at it. You have to learn the right skills and practice them regularly until emotional awareness turns into a habit. The more emotional awareness becomes habitual, the easier it will be to take care of our emotional life and feel less controlled or overwhelmed by them.

Here's where my action guide can help you become more aware of your emotions.

1.   Name your emotions, write them down and identify themes

You may find it silly to read this. But you don't always know what you are feeling. None of us do. What you or anyone feels involves a mix of discrete, nuanced, and subtle shades of feelings.

If your partner tells a joke about you at a dinner party, you'll likely feel embarrassed. You might also notice that you feel angry. Underneath the anger and embarrassment, you might even feel sadness and disappointment. You might begin to ask: "Is the joke a signal that my partner doesn't care about my feelings? Will my partner abandon me? Does my partner love me?" Those kinds of fears are primal and far from uncommon, but it can be difficult to admit you have them, let alone take the time to care for them.

You may harbor murky feelings that you find difficult to define, let alone express. If you're in that boat, use a dictionary or thesaurus. Discover new words to describe what you are experiencing. Maybe you think you feel nervous but you're actually feeling apprehensive. You might think what you're experiencing is disappointment, but it might more accurately be described as dismay.

Don't limit yourself to single words. Use phrases and idioms and sentences describe how you feel. Use similes and metaphors. Add details about the ways your body is reacting to the feeling. Write everything down.

When you're satisfied with all the descriptions you've gathered, take a close look at them. Identify which ones are your key emotions. Which feelings are crucial for you right now?

Don't think too much. Limit yourself to three seconds. In that way, your intuition, instead of your intellect, will guide your choice.

In doing this exercise, you'll access your skills in language. By labeling feelings, you'll fine-tune your perception. You'll deepen your understanding. You'll get in touch with how you truly feel.

2. Track one of your key emotions throughout the day in a journal

Using your intuition, pick one key emotion from your list.

If you pick "fear," how often do you feel afraid throughout the day? Write it down. Describe what you fear. Ask yourself why you feel afraid. What were you doing when you felt that fear? Who were you with? What were they doing or saying? Where were you in relation to them?

Notes like those will help you get a better grasp of your fear. Eventually you'll have a fear "portfolio." You'll use it to identify triggers. Next time there's a trigger, you'll see it for what it is. You'll have done the background work to develop a healthier response to it.

If you're like most people, you'll write down a lot of negative feelings. Our evolutionary brain pays attention to negative feelings.[90] Neuroscientists call it negativity bias. The brain unconsciously interprets negative feelings as a sign of a potential danger. In an act of self-preservation, the brain naturally gives more attention to negative emotions. That's why it's important to track your positive emotions as well.

Write down in your journal every time you feel happy throughout the day. Note what you are doing and who you are with. Develop your happiness "portfolio." It will help you identify where and when you feel most content. You can repeat the activities that make you happy. You'll learn to engage in those happy activities in a way that is more emotionally aware. Also, recent research in neuroscience suggests that writing down what you feel grateful for daily for as little as three weeks will help boost happiness and result in better sleep and more energy.[91] Try that, too!

3. Cope with negative emotions in positive ways

Everyone experiences negative feelings. They are part of life. It's hard to imagine a world without negative feelings. While they're unpleasant, they're necessary. Feeling sorrow enables us to feel joy. More importantly, negative feelings can reveal our deepest unfulfilled desires. They can push us to take care of our needs.

Negative feelings tend to arise because we've made negative associations with something, often unconsciously. If you have negative feelings about dogs—fear, disgust and anger—it may be that you've associated dogs with unpleasant things like biting, barking, or tearing up your garden. But if you begin to see dogs in positive ways—as playful and loving—you'll develop new associations.

If you picked "fear" as your key emotion, widespread contagions and epidemics like COVID-19 might be a trigger. When you think about COVID-19, you might worry about your health and financial security. On its own, COVID-19 cannot take responsibility for your fear. Only you can. The meanings you attach to illness play a significant part in how you feel about it.

Fear often arises in times of uncertainty. When things are uncertain, no one knows what will happen next. But if all you can imagine is all the terrible things that could happen, your fear will control you. If you take time to imagine the positive things that might come out of uncertainty, you'll develop new associations with, and new meanings for, uncertain times.

Instead of brooding on all the doom and gloom, consider the ways that uncertain situations—like the pandemic—offer hope and possibility. In the case of COVID-19, health has become a global priority. If you've started exercising daily to stay healthy, appreciate that. Ask what creative opportunities the pandemic brings to your work or business. If you still find yourself stuck in doom and gloom, revisit chapter four. Take a closer look at the story you tell yourself. Write a new one.

4. Practice mindfulness daily

Mindfulness takes many forms. Deep yawning, slow stretching, gentle caressing.[92] Choose a mindfulness activity that you enjoy and that works. That will enable you to create space around strong feelings or sensations. It will enable you to quickly change your state of mind.

Practice mindfulness every 20, 30, or 40 minutes. Find out what works for you. Download a mindfulness bell on your phone or computer to remind you when it's time to be mindful. You'll train yourself to be more aware of both your bodily sensations and emotional states in the moment. You'll learn to get in touch with your emotions and stay in tune with them.

The benefits of mindfulness are often immediate, but it takes daily practice over time to make awareness an ingrained habit. Over time, mindfulness can help you to take care of your feelings and become more engaged in your own life.[93] When you can do that, you can take care of others' emotions, too.

You can also use the term "emotional intelligence," first coined by two psychologists John Mayer and Peter Salavoy and popularized by Daniel Goleman in his 1995 book of the same name, to describe emotional awareness.[94] A high degree of emotional intelligence enables you to care for your emotions and prevent the occurrence of negative feelings, especially strong, spontaneous, and uncontrollable ones. Emotional intelligence can help you avoid doing things you'll later regret.

For example, if you're a parent and you walk into the living room and see your two-year old drawing a rainbow on your expensive carpet with a permanent marker, imagine how mindfulness, along with emotional intelligence, can change your response. Mindfulness enables you to stay calm.

Remaining calm will benefit both your well-being and that of the child. Besides, getting angry won't help in cleaning the carpet.

If you're a teacher, you'll know that screaming at your students when they misbehave doesn't work in the long term. Instead, an unruly classroom presents an opportunity to explore what lies beneath the disruptive behavior. If you're in a relationship, the ability to accept your partner's negative emotions and nurture what lies beneath them can often improve the quality of your connection. The same is true of any relationship.

When you're emotionally aware, you can cope with whatever life throws at you. A life of peace, happiness, and fulfillment depends on it.

In Summary

Language triggers emotions. Emotions dictate our thoughts and behavior. But language plays a more profound role in how we perceive and experience emotions than we'd assumed. Adults can regulate their emotions through higher levels of cognition in the use of language.

Here are some of the most important points I discussed in the chapter:

- Speaking in a foreign language can mitigate the intensity of our feelings and emotions.
- Language acts like a telescope that brings vague feelings into focus.
- Language gives form and structure to abstract constructs. Emotions are abstractions constructs as well. By naming emotions, you shape the perception and experience of your feelings.
- There's only a limited number of feelings we can perceive; There's inadequacy of single words to articulate our emotions.
- Emotions, like languages, are shaped by culture. Different cultures use different concepts and constructs to express feelings, and even universally-understood terms like "love" are shaped by traditions of different cultures.

- Using language to label feelings can help mitigate the phobias and stress.

In the end, I provided an action guide to help you get in touch with your emotions and find peace and happiness. This guide harnesses the power of language in regulating emotions by integrating mindfulness (an important strategy in Neurocoaching) with the help of words. To become emotionally aware is the key to take care of your emotional life. But it is not something that our brains are hard-wired to do. That's why we have to work at it and practice it daily. The effect won't come to you overnight, but if you stick to it for at least a week, you'll begin to see substantial benefits of such practice.

Chapter 6: What Does Language Have to do with Learning and Self-development?

"Philosophy is a battle against the bewitchment of our intelligence by means of our language."

Ludwig Wittgenstein[95]

"A man with a scant vocabulary will almost certainly be a weak thinker. The richer and more copious one's vocabulary and the greater one's awareness of fine distinctions and subtle nuances of meaning, the more fertile and precise is likely to be one's thinking. Knowledge of things and knowledge of the words for them grow together. If you do not know the words, you do not know the things."

Henry Hazlitt[96]

K nowledge is power. In an age of a constant change and disruption, no one can dispute the importance of learning.

But what is behind your desire to learn? Are you motivated to simply know more? To accomplish more? To become a better person?

How does learning happen? And what role does learning play in your self-development?

Learning is a social activity. We learn when we communicate with others, when we interact with knowledge, and when we exchange ideas. Whether we communicate with teachers, friends or random strangers on the street, each exchange with each individual can teach us something. We also earn from books, newspapers, magazines and television shows. You may read or watch TV alone, but there is a social element to engaging with another person's knowledge, stories, and images. When you watch a film or read a book, you converse with its ideas. You interpret whatever you read or watch. In that sense, a dialog emerges between you and the source you are learning from.

We are learning all the time. But learning is only possible with the assistance of language. We use language to understand new information, to make sense of our conversations and to communicate the ideas we've acquired. Our ability to learn is largely influenced by our ability to read, listen, empathize, and communicate.

For an engine to have power, it needs fuel. If knowledge is power, language is the fuel.

How does language affect thinking?

In his 2013 paper, Professor of education Robert Coe from Durham University defined the secret of learning as "Learning happens when you think hard."[97]

If it's true that you need to "think hard" to learn, and if language enables you to "think" in the first place, then it follows that language plays an important role in learning.

But to what extent does language affect the quality of your thinking and your ability to learn?

Directed by Denis Villneuve and written by Eric Heissener, the 2016 film *Arrival* explores both of those questions. Adapted for screen from Ted Chiang's 2002 science fiction novella *Story of Your Life*, *Arrival* asks whether the way we represent experience reflects how we experience time. Played by Amy Adams, Dr. Louise Banks is a world-class linguist. The US military asks her to decode the language of an extra-terrestrial species that has just landed on Earth. When Louise meets the aliens—two giant squid-like beasts with seven tentacles—she and her colleague name the pair "Abbott" and "Costello."

Louise can't make sense of the alien's speech, but she has better luck with the alien form of writing, which whirls in elegant circles from their webbed hands. Louise understands each circle as a fully formed sentence, one with neither a clear beginning nor end. She learns that the aliens see the universe in a way that is fundamentally different to the way we do. When we form sentences, we generally write them down in a straight line. Left to right, right to left or top to bottom. When we think of time, most of us think of it running along a straight line: Past to present to future. But as Louise begins to make sense of the alien syntax, her perception of time shifts. She learns to see time in a non-linear way; She begins to have visions of the past and future.

Before Ted Chiang wrote *Story of Your Life*, he spent five years researching linguistics. His depiction of Louise's shifting perception of reality suggests that Chiang might have been influenced by a popular theory in the field of linguistics: The Sapir–Whorf hypothesis.

In a nutshell, the Sapir–Whorf hypothesis suggests that the language we speak either fully determines or strongly influences our thoughts. Not everyone agrees. Noam Chomsky argues that all languages share certain grammatical characteristics. He thinks that there exists a universal, innate, and unlearned structure of human language.[98] Linguist and cognitive scientist Steven Pinker claims that the structure of language—grammar for example—comes primarily from what he calls a "language instinct," which is determined by our genes.[99]

But despite its critics, in the past two decades, the Sapir–Whorf hypothesis has been supported by interdisciplinary research. In 2010, psychologists Phillip Wolff and Kevin J. Holmes identified seven ways that language affects thinking. Those include the ways we think about motion, color, spatial relations, numbers, and false beliefs.[100] In 2004, brain scientist Daniel Casasanto, linguist Lera Boroditssky, and anthropologist David Gil collaborated in an attempt to uncover the relationship between thinking and speaking. They found that English and Indonesian speakers tend to map their sense of the duration of time in a linear way. Both languages use expressions like: "In a long time." Greek and Spanish speakers represent time as quantity rather than distance. They say: "In much time." That suggests that the metaphors we use to represent time may profoundly influence our perspective of time.[101]

Another influential theory of the relationship between thinking and speaking comes from the Soviet psychologist Lev Vygotsky. In his 1934 book *Thought and Language*, he proposes that when children develop skills in language, they depend on the guidance and assistance of adults. He called that process "scaffolding."[102]

Think of when workmen construct an apartment building. Builders often use a structure of wooden planks and metal poles outside the developing building, or what's called a scaffolding. In the earliest stages of development, a building needs that outside support. In the early stages of language development, children also need outside support. They need adults to structure and support the ways that language is used.

Vygotsky argues that speech also plays an important role in children's ability to solve problems. When children say things aloud, it helps to guide and focus their attention. A child will often repeat and rehearse phrases with the outside support, or guidance, of an adult. If you have experience with young toddlers, you may have noticed how often they talk to themselves. If an adult instructs a child, that child will often repeat those instructions aloud when they're playing games.

Influenced by Vygotsky, in 1992 Laura E. Berk and Rafael Diaz published *Private Speech: From Social Interaction to Self-regulation*.[103] Their research shows that children tend to talk to themselves when a task is particularly complicated. They also discovered that children who talk to themselves tend to have higher success rates when it comes to solving problems.

The role that language plays in solving problems is not only apparent in children. It appears in adults. Have you ever talked to yourself when you were dealing with a challenging task? Saying things aloud helps to focus your attention. Your voice guides you through the steps you need to take. Saying things aloud helps you think clearly. That's why people use post-it notes. Writing an idea down on a post-it is similar to talking about the idea to yourself. Putting your process into words helps you organize your thoughts.

Many contemporary theorists have discredited the hypothesis that language fully determines how we think. But the idea that language *influences* thought is disputed by few.

But is all human thought dependent on language?

You may have had the experience of thinking without words. When you see a picture of a rich, dense forest, it might trigger you to imagine what is happening in that forest. The root of the word "imagination" is "image." We can "think" in images, without the use of words.

Have you ever had an "aha" moment? That's when an insight instantaneously arrives. Often "aha" moments come to us unaccompanied by language. The words you use to describe that instantaneous insight usually come later. Language helps you develop and apply that insight. Fast, unconscious thought does not involve language.

But there are certain types of thought that would be inaccessible without language.

Logical reasoning requires language. It happens slowly and consciously, rather than quickly and unconsciously. Animals don't have access to language, so they can't reason in the way that humans can. Logic is believed to be related to consciousness. Non-logical processes in the brain are mostly unconscious.

Brain scientists use the terms "vague-unconscious" and "crisp-conscious" to describe the ways our thinking moves from vague and unconscious representations toward crisp and conscious thoughts[104]. That helps explain the interaction between language and cognition. Language is mostly conscious; cognition is rarely so.

Does learning a second language make you smarter?

In *Arrival*, it's certainly true that learning a second language—in this case an alien's—gives Louise insight that most humans can't access. Learning an alien's language shifts her perception of time. It changes the ways she perceives the world. It alters the way she experiences life.

Critics have suggested that the movie takes the popular theory of language too far. Even if the Sapir–Whorf hypothesis has merit, is it possible to radically shift the way you think about life simply by learning a new language? What do you think? What potential do you think lies in learning an additional language?

I think radical transformation through language learning is possible. Ted Chiang drew inspiration for his novella from the vibrational principle in physics. Predictions from science fiction have often come true. Our first moon landing, the existence of submarines, and the ubiquity of mobile phones all had their existence in fiction long before they appeared in real life.

But the value of his story does not lie solely in the depiction of the radical transformation of one woman's life. Both the film *Arrival* and the novella *Story of Your Life* invite us to rethink what language is to us and what it might bring us.

In the first part, I shared that when I learned a second language—in my case English—it changed how I perceived and experienced life, both in tangible and intangible ways.

But does that experience make me smarter?

Let's just say that at least it made me feel smarter.

There are times when I talk to myself in English, especially when I need to make a difficult decision. Speaking in a foreign language helps me view a situation more rationally. Speaking in English gives clarity to my thoughts because I feel less controlled by my emotions. My students say they like the way I encourage discussion by asking in-depth questions, and they are constantly amazed by my fresh perspectives. My friends say I use strong logical reasoning even in small chat.

If you're bilingual, you might have experienced some of the above. Even if you don't, chances are you may have experienced the struggle to find the right word to describe something in your first language. You might have relied on your second language instead. If you raise your child in a bilingual environment, I bet you've seen that child mixing languages. It is common for children growing up with two languages, or even bilingual adults, to select words and phrases that work better in each language. As a parent, you might panic at the thought of your child learning less of one language when she adopts a new one.

Empirical research demonstrates the opposite is true. A study by Agnes Kovacs in 2009 measured the amount of language infants learn. Bilingual infants learn exactly the same amount of language in two languages as their monolingual peers do in one. They learn the same words, or the same vocabulary, in both languages[105].

More recent research demonstrates that, contrary to the view that bilingualism complicates the two language systems—the building blocks and structure of the two languages—the two languages become part of the same system. When a bilingual person speaks, both languages are simultaneously active. That might seem obvious when someone is speaking in a second language. If you French is your second language, your mother tongue remains active when you speak French. But the same is true when you speak in your mother tongue—French remains active in your mind. That explains why sometimes bilingual individuals struggle to find the right word in their native tongue but easily come up with the right word in their adopted language. It also explains my own distinct feeling that my second language affects how I speak my native tongue.

Bilingual people learn to regulate their use of both languages. Their brain learns to control the activation of each language, reducing the activation of one when the other is in use. That has an overall effect on the brain. Since the brain is constantly regulating its use of language, it learns to more readily control its responses to experience. Research suggests that bilingual people more easily filter out irrelevant information, switch between tasks and resolve situations where there involves conflicts.

Studies by Pascale Engel de Abreu, Director of the Language and Cognitive Development group at the University of Luxembourg, showed that bilingual students perform control tasks better.[106] These tasks require selective attention and the elimination of interference. Bilingual students are better at focusing while filtering out irrelevant information. They are also better at problem-solving and switching between tasks. Those qualities, known as executive functions of the brain, are largely determined by the dorsolateral prefrontal cortex. For bilinguals, the attention and effort required to switch between languages triggers more activity in this region of the brain and can potentially strengthen its function.

According to Sam Wang, a neuroscientist at Princeton University, children exposed to two languages demonstrate better abilities to resolve conflicting cues and perform on Stroop tests. The Stroop test presents a mismatch or conflict between the name of a color and the color the word is printed in. For example, the word "red" might be printed in blue ink instead of red. The test demonstrates cognitive interference where there is a delay in the reaction time on a task due to a mismatch in stimuli.[107]

Why do bilinguals perform better at tasks where there are cognitive conflicts? Each language has its own rules and frames. When you work within one set of rules and frames, you exercise one mental set. When the rules of a new language come into conflict with the rules of your native tongue, you have to unlearn the old rules to learn the new ones. It is just like learning to ride a tricycle after you've been riding a bicycle. You learn how to ride a tricycle almost immediately as a child. But if you've been riding a bicycle, you'll find it challenging to ride a tricycle. The rules and mental sets required in riding these two types of vehicles are different. You need to let go of the rules of riding two wheels before you can learn to ride three.

Bilinguals, especially those who have been bilingual for long periods in their lives, are constantly regulating and switching between different rules and frames. Years of "exercise" make their brains supple and agile. That explains why being a lifetime bilingual helps to delay symptoms of diseases like Alzheimer's and dementia, according to Ellen Bialystok, Research Professor of Psychology and Walter Gordon York Research Chair of Lifespan Cognitive Development at York University in Canada.[108] It helps that when you speak two languages, you exercise more of your brain.

Neuroimaging studies have demonstrated that a bilingual brain looks different from that of a monolingual. It has a higher density of grey matter, a higher integrity of white matter, and a larger cortical thickness and volume. Second-language learning induces neuroplasticity at the macrostructural level, though a recent study showed that this benefit is closely related with the age of acquiring a second language. Early acquisition is more beneficial than acquisition at adulthood.[109]

But there are certainly benefits for adults who learn a second language. Research shows that bilingual adults exhibit less emotional bias and approach problems in their second language more rationally than in their native language. That explains why my student cursed in his second language to let go of his frustration and why I prefer to make difficult decisions with the help of my second language.

If all that sounds exciting to you, why not learn another language? It is never too late for your brain to start a new language routine, just as it is never too late for your body to start a new workout routine. Structural neuroplasticity is associated with learning, of any kind, because learning something new is based on the capacity of the brain to adapt to new experiences. We can argue that learning a new language increases that capacity.

How does language improve your efforts in self-development?

Have you ever heard about the "language gap" or "word gap"? It refers to the difference in linguistic environment between wealthy families and those who live in poverty. This produces a gap in language outcome that contributes to children's trajectory toward educational success or failure.[110] The debate over the relationship of language, socio-economic class, and education has been going on in academic and popular discourse since the 1960s.

While there is no fixed solution to bridge this "language gap," it is important for us to be aware of the role that language plays in learning.[111] By learning, I do not only mean the kind of learning that takes place in a classroom for students, but also, and more importantly, learning that happens in a more informal setting among adults. We now live in a time of rapid change. Everyone needs to learn in order to survive and thrive. Otherwise, you risk stagnation; you end up doing the same thing and expecting the same results. I bet you do not want that to happen. But you might wonder: How do words and language help with learning and self-development?

As discussed in chapter four, the language you use in your daily life shapes your perception of reality and your inner life. A farmer speaks a language of crops, insects, and pesticides. An investor speaks a language of portfolio, returns, and assessment. A neuroscientist speaks a language of neural networks and brain structures. An educator speaks a language of meaning-making, understanding and internalization. All of these professions use their own concepts and distinctions. They use their own words to discuss the themes, topics, and notions that distinguish them in their fields. How individuals use language often distinguishes an expert from an insider from a layman.

Language supports our concepts and distinctions of the world. It gives us the idea of a tree and distinguishes a yew from a pine. Language supports knowledge. Language supports theories of particles in physics and ideas of irony in theater. When researchers, artists, and thinkers illuminate a concept that has not yet been fully understood, they are contributing to knowledge.

But when someone contributes a new idea to a field of knowledge, it's difficult to describe that idea in clear, readily available and readily understood language. Theorists explain certain phenomena by coming up with the language to explain it. But that language can be difficult to understand until it has been integrated and accepted widely.

As an educator, I have always believed the importance of focusing on students' strengths and bringing out the best in them. I seldom criticize my students. I believe criticism kills creativity. But I don't always know how to realize those beliefs in my teaching.

When I read about the theory of appreciative inquiry, a window opened in my mind. I learned that my beliefs had been backed up by an established theory. Reading about appreciative inquiry helped me translate my beliefs into my teaching practice. While I'm amazed by the beauty of the theory, I sometimes wonder why I didn't come up with it myself! The truth is, I didn't yet have the conceptual language.

Think about an experience of being in a crowd, like a jam-packed sports stadium. You may have noticed that people in the crowd act a lot like each other. It might have even made you feel uncomfortable or influenced you to behave differently than you normally would. But if you read theories of herding behavior, you'll understand that you're not alone in your experience. People in a crowd tend to behave like one another. Armed with that knowledge, the next time you find yourself in a crowd, you'll be able to exercise critical thinking.

If you want to improve your learning, one way to start is to read up on theories of how to learn best. If you read that learning is social, for example, that it happens through interaction, you'll likely make a point of exchanging ideas with people whenever you can. As you increase your vocabulary, you'll have a richer toolbox in which to see, interpret, and represent the world.

So, what other practical ways can you increase your knowledge and develop your skills in learning?

First, read more. Read about anything that interests you. When you read more, your literacy improves at the same time. Research shows that learning to read transforms our brain.[112] The brain network that crosses your frontal, temporal and parietal regions is activated when you process words in any language.[113]

Second, find ways to increase your vocabulary. Extending your vocabulary will help you develop insights into areas of your life you don't usually pay attention to. If what you pay attention to represents your reality, extending your vocabulary will expand your view of reality. The more you pay attention to, the greater your engagement with life will be. Extending your emotional vocabulary will also help you perceive the world with greater clarity. There is evidence from research that suggests that children who are explicitly taught emotional concepts in school perform better on a range of social, emotional, and educational outcomes.[114]

There's further benefits in building a larger vocabulary. It can help you succeed in your career.

If you have ever communicated with high-level executives, you might notice that they communicate with a significantly higher-level vocabulary than other professionals. They speak clearly, and they use more descriptive, intelligent, and sometimes more conceptual words to articulate their ideas. According to Johnson O'Connor, President of Harvard's Human Engineering Lab, "Words are the instruments, by means of which, men and women grasp the thoughts of others and which they do much of their own thinking. They are the tools of thought." [115]

Studies at the Human Engineering Laboratory at Stevens Institute of Technology tracked thousands of successful people from all fields and disciplines, and they found one common trait that is shared by all of them: they have all acquired a large vocabulary.[116] There are more studies that prove the direct link between vocabulary size and success. In a notable study conducted by the Johnson O'Connor Research Foundation (JORF), managerial professionals from 39 companies were given a vocabulary test. The results showed a "direct correlation between vocabulary size and rank on the corporate ladder."[117]

Experiments and tests done over the past decades also show that no matter the profession—engineering, management or media—a good vocabulary is the best predictor for career success. Moreover, results have shown that the large vocabulary usually comes before achievement, rather than a result of it.

Some neuro tips to pump up your learning

In traditional learning and teaching, knowledge is most often the focus. In an educational context, learners focus on remembering knowledge. Tests focus on the testing of knowledge. Teachers focus on the transmission of knowledge. But there are things that are more important than knowledge. Imagination, inspiration, creativity, and innovation are all important. Everyone's brain has the potential to be imaginative, inspired, and innovative. And when you're imaginative, inspired, and innovative, you'll learn faster.

The following neuro tips will help you get in touch with your brain's potential and learn at your best:

1. Prepare yourself mentally before you engage with a learning task. Good preparation helps you concentrate and prevents you from getting distracted. Relax your mind and body through the mindfulness strategies that I introduced in an earlier chapter. You can also meditate for a few minutes as well as practice affirmations around the purpose of your learning. Focus on how learning connects with your highest values and the positive results that it will bring.

   For example, your affirmations might sound like this: "Today I'm learning about appreciative inquiry, which gives me power and helps me become the educator I want to be. To achieve this goal, I'm committed to hours of persistent, focused, and consistent learning." When your sense of meaning and purpose increase, your stress levels drop dramatically.

2. Take notes whenever you can. When you come across a useful idea, take note of it. By translating what you learn into your own words, you'll engage more. And when you engage more with the material,

your brain will remain active. As a result, whatever you learn has a greater chance to inspire you.

If you have time, share your notes with friends. By sharing, you'll engage in a dialog with others. It will force you to clarify concepts in your own words. You'll arrive at a deeper understanding of the things you learn when you share them with others.

3. Be playful with your learning. Have fun. Take whatever measures you can to make sure you enjoy the learning process. You can use a different learning method than you would usually use. You can create a piece of artwork to present your learning outcome—like a painting, a mind map or a poem. You can create a game to play with friends. Playfulness and fun are food for creativity.

4. Take mindful breaks. Use a mindfulness bell to ring twice or three times each hour. When the bell rings, take a break to practice mindfulness. You can practice mindfulness strategies that we talked about in earlier chapters or whatever things that bring you pleasure.

By doing that, your brain will be refreshed, and you'll be able to access your intuition, which leads the way to those "aha" moments. Mindfulness helps with your efficiency. Research done by Mark Waldman and his colleagues at Loyola Marymount University in Los Angeles, with students at Executive MBA program, have shown that brain-based mindfulness techniques not only speed up the learning process, but they also boost work productivity and teamwork cooperation while reducing physical and emotional stress.

In Summary

Learning is only possible with the assistance of language. We use language to understand new information, to make sense of our conversations, and to communicate the ideas we acquired. What role does language play in our learning and self-development? I proposed the following ideas:

- Language plays a scaffolding role in the way that it guides problem-solving for both children and adults. It also helps us focus attention.
- Logical reasoning requires the use of language, which happens slowly and consciously, rather than quickly and unconsciously, like when an insight instantaneously arrives.
- Bilinguals perform better at tasks where there are cognitive conflicts since their brains are constantly regulating the use of two languages, the rules and structures of which are usually in conflict. Thanks to years of "exercise" of the brain, they experience diseases like Alzheimer's and dementia later in their lives than their counterparts.
- Second language learning induces neuroplasticity at the macrostructural level.
- Language supports our concepts and distinctions of the world. If you don't have the conceptual language for something, you hardly have any knowledge about something. Likewise, if you increase your vocabulary, you'll have a richer toolbox in which to see, interpret, and represent the world. Research shows a direct correlation between vocabulary size and rank on the corporate ladder.

I gave, at the end, neurotips for you to develop a healthier brain and pump up your learning. You can start with the ones that appeal to you the most before applying the others in your learning. If you practice these tips for a week, you will begin to appreciate their beauty and keep practicing them until they become ingrained habits.

Part 3

How Can You Use the Power of Language to Change Your Life

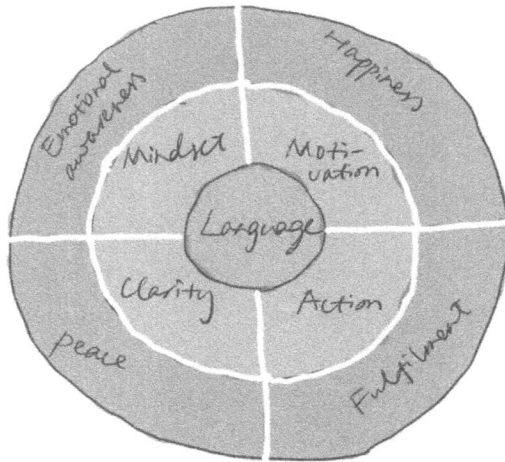

Figure 5

In part one, I shared with you my story of transformation brought by language. You may have noticed I harnessed the power of language to achieve clarity, shift mindset, get motivated, and take actions. Chapter six highlighted the crucial role of emotional awareness in cultivating peace, happiness, and fulfillment. The diagram (*figure 5*) is a full integration of all these elements while showcasing their links with each other.

Drawing from my own experience and recent advances in research, I identified four key elements (clarity, mindset, motivation, and action) and created action guides that integrate the best use of language with Neurocoaching strategies. The three chapters in this part walk you through the action steps that allow you to change your life and manifest the life you desire.

Chapter 7: Gain Clarity and Live by Your Values

"The secret of genius is to carry the spirit of the child into old age, which means never losing your enthusiasm."

Aldous Huxley[118]

What are your deepest inner values? Chances are that you might not have a solid answer right away. Values can be abstract and elusory; they can be hard to define.

It might be easier to begin by identifying your passions. What are they? Do you have any?

You've likely been asked that question so many times that by now it's turned into a cliché. Or maybe you think passions are worth thinking about but find them difficult to translate into any practical activity. Some people feel comfortable living their lives without following their passions. Others have a clear idea on what they're most passionate about but are content not to pursue it. And then there are the few who think that living without the pursuit of a passion is unthinkable.

If you have a passion, are you pursuing it actively? Or are you content to live without it?

For Charles Strickland, a main character in W. Somerset Maugham's novel *The Moon and the Sixpence,* a life without passion is unimaginable.[119] Maugham based the character on the life of the post-impressionist painter Paul Gauguin. Like Gauguin, Strickland is a well-heeled, middle-aged English businessman who finds middle-class life in London suffocating. Intent on following his passions, Strickland abandons his wife and family, moves to Paris and devotes himself single-mindedly to art and beauty. Throwing away convention, he leaves the security and comfort of his affluent lifestyle and spends his days as a painter living in appalling poverty and degradation.

In the eyes of English society, Strickland has fallen from grace. He is an irresponsible husband and father and an ungrateful friend. He's a womanizer. He is misanthropic and apathetic. He's a destructive genius who frequently acts with hostility to those around him. But despite his misdemeanors, hostility, and poverty, Strickland finds a sense of fulfillment, meaning, and beauty in the pursuit of his passion for painting.

Isn't it romantic to imagine yourself living a life in pursuit of passion no matter the cost? Most people don't go to the extremes that Strickland does to follow a dream. For many of us, Strickland is not a role model, but he's certainly an intriguing fictional character.

In real life, many creative people have taken tremendous risks in the pursuit of their passions. Harrison Ford traded in a relatively stable life of a carpenter to embrace the tumultuous life of an actor. Steve Jobs dropped out of college and spent months living in India to uncover what he wanted to do with his life. In her 2008 Harvard commencement speech, J.K. Rowling said, "I was convinced that the only thing I ever wanted to do was to write novels. However, my parents, both of whom came from impoverished backgrounds and neither of whom had been to college, took the view that my overactive imagination was an amusing personal quirk that would never pay a mortgage, or secure a pension."[120] Rowling wrote *Harry Potter in the Philosopher's Stone* in between the poorly-paid English lessons she taught to Portuguese students. A single mother, she lived on a shoestring budget. But her tenacity paid off; she is now one of the most successful living writers in the world.

To Harrison Ford, Steve Jobs, and J.K. Rowling, following a passion represented something more fruitful than following a fortune. Perhaps one difference between intensely passionate people and the rest of us is that those with passion believe there is no other choice but to follow their dreams. Their passions are not hobbies but are keys to who they truly are. They define how they lead their lives. For many people, a life lived without the pursuit of a passion is perfectly acceptable. But for extraordinarily passionate people, to not follow a dream and become who they must be would render life intolerable. It would be more dreadful than poverty. Following a passion for some can be the difference between living a mediocre life and one full of meaning and purpose.

You may not have a passion. Or you may not be pursuing your passion right now. You may have an inkling of what you want to do with your life, but the details might be hazy. As a child, you likely had an answer ready when someone inevitably asked you: "What do you want to be when you grow up?" As an adult, do you still have that answer ready?

You might want to become an entrepreneur, a mentor, a speaker, a mother, or a father. But if I ask you to name one thing that defines you, chances are that you won't be able answer immediately. You may have to explore more. Even us grownups at times have yet to discover who we truly are, what we truly love and what we must become. A lot of us have to yet discover what that person looks like. If you're in the dark, don't worry. You're not alone.

The late American poet Mary Oliver ends her poem "The Summer Day" with a similar question: "Tell me, what is it you plan to do with your one wild and precious life?"[121] Knowing what you plan to do with your "one wild and precious life" comes down to knowing who you truly are and what you have to do to live a life you desire. It motivates you to overcome any challenges you face on your path. Knowledge of who you truly are can act as the north star that navigates your ship through its darkest nights. When you do that, your true self appears in everything you do. When you are aware of who you truly are, that person can steer the decisions you make in your daily life. The little things you do every day affect your overall well-being. When everything you do echoes your truest self—that person who knows what she has to do with her life—you'll feel more peaceful and more content. But when what you do comes into conflict with who you truly are, you'll struggle.

Making your path clear first means establishing a strong understanding of who you are. You need to know what makes you happy. You need to know what kind life you value and what you truly desire. You need to decide what is most essential to your life. To tune into your true north—your truest self, the navigator that is always present—all you require is clarity about what makes you uniquely you. Achieving that clarity enables you to strip away the inessential things in life so that you can invest in what truly matters. Awareness of what's essential provides the foundation of a life lived with a strong sense of meaning and purpose.

Sometimes, it takes setbacks and failures to arrive at a sense of clarity about who you truly are and what's important to you. As J.K. Rowling said in her Harvard speech:

> "I had failed on an epic scale. An exceptionally short-lived marriage had imploded, and I was jobless, a lone parent, and as poor as it is possible to be in modern Britain, without being homeless...failure meant a stripping away of the inessential. I stopped pretending to myself that I was anything other than what I was, and I began to direct all my energy into finishing the only work that mattered to me. Had I really succeeded at anything else, I might never have found the determination to succeed in the one arena I believed I truly belonged." 122

Think of a time you failed. Did it help you achieve a sense of clarity? If not, don't worry. Try the following instead.

Step One: Elicit your value words, the most powerful words in your life.

Before arriving at a strong understanding of yourself—what makes you happy, what kind of life you truly desire and what makes you *you*—the first step is establishing an understanding of what you value most. Your value words can be the most powerful words in your life. They help you figure out what you truly want and who you truly are.

To recognize your value words, begin telling a story about a favorite character from history, literature, film, television, or the present day. When you write your story, ask *Why do I like that character?* If you cannot come up with a character, think about the qualities that you admire most and use those to help think of someone who clearly embodies those qualities.

Write a story about that character. Or you can talk about the character with a friend and record your conversation. If you like, you can do both. You'll find benefits in each of those methods of inquiry.

Here's what a friend narrated to me when I posed the question to her.

> The qualities that I admire are perseverance, resilience, forgiveness, generosity, and integrity. So, my character will have all these qualities. The character that comes to mind now is Joan of Arc. She was so courageous (1). She stood out in her time (2). She was a girl (3) at a time when it was still a man's world (3). Just imagine how much more it was a man's world in her era. The thing I admire about her is that she had visions at a time when it was dangerous (1) to tell people that you had visions. If you did, you would end up dead (1). But she was not afraid (1). That is inspiring to me. Joan of Arc was not afraid to go out into the world and do what her vision told her to do (1) even though it might have been dangerous (1). And actually, she did go to war (1) because her vision told her to. She rode a white horse, and she led an assault to defend her country (1). She was still a young girl (1, 3). Yet somehow her beliefs inspired people around her, and people followed her (2). She gave them hope (2, 4). She gave them purpose (2, 4). She made them believe that they could succeed (2). Those are the things that I see in her. Her courage (1) and her beliefs might not have been widely influential, but they still inspired many (2). For some, her visions posed a threat (1). As I am speaking to you, I realize that I am talking about myself (1). I was talking about her beliefs being a threat (1). That's my fear—that I will be criticized or put down (1). But that is exactly what [Joan of Arc] went through (1). She received visions. She believed those visions. And she stayed true to them to the end until the end of her life (5). She never wavered (5).

By studying the underlined parts closely, you can identify the value words. I organized what I noticed into a table.

Courage (1)	so courageous; she was a girl; she had visions at a time when it was dangerous; you would end up dead; but she wasn't afraid; she was not afraid to go out into the world with her vision; it might have been dangerous; actually, she did go to war; she rode a white horse and led an assault to defend her country; she was still a young girl; her courage; then for others, it was a threat; I was talking about myself; her beliefs being a threat; my fear that I will be criticized or put down; but that is exactly what [Joan of Arc] went through;
Leadership (2)	stood out in her time; her beliefs so inspired the world; gave them purpose; gave them hope; around her that they followed her; made them believe that they could win; even though her beliefs might not have been widely influential, they inspired many;
Female Empowerment (3)	she was a girl; at a time when it was still a man's world; she was still a young girl;
Generosity (4)	gave them hope; gave them purpose;
Perseverance (5)	she received visions. She believed those visions. She stayed true to them until the end of her life; she never wavered

My friend clearly values courage. She uses the word "courageous" in her introductory sentences, and the phrase "not afraid" appears more than once. She refers to Joan of Arc's uprightness in her religious beliefs, a position that required tremendous courage in the 15th century. She mentions a few of Joan of Arc's courageous acts. Joan of Arc went "to war" and "led an assault to defend her country." To counteract her own fears of criticism, my friend says that like Joan of Arc, she also needs courage.

She also points out that Joan of Arc was as a young girl and that she had to dress up as a boy to fight. That suggests that female empowerment might also be a value for her. She speaks about how Joan of Arc gave her people hope that they would win the war. Joan of Arc led the French army and boosted their morale; both of those are traits of great leaders. Generosity and leadership may be key values for my friend, too.

In addition to courage, female empowerment, generosity, and leadership, my friend values perseverance. She points out that Joan of Arc stayed true to her beliefs "to the end of her life" and "never wavered." Joan of Arc persevered.

You might ascribe different value words to my friend's story, but her innermost values remain constant, whichever words you choose to describe them. Those value words represent what she wants to embody in her own life. In other words, her value words describe who she is at her core.

When I was talking about these value words to my friend, she said they revealed clues about her true self. She explained it the following way:

- Courage: I always feel fear in my heart. Fear about not being good enough. Fear about how my business might not appeal to my target clients. I want to release the fear and accomplish my goals.
- Leadership: I've never thought that leadership might become a core value of mine. But since you mentioned it, I think it's always been there. Subconsciously, I've always wanted to lead and influence others.
- Generosity: I want to give and serve, both in my daily life and in my business.
- Female empowerment: Like the value of leadership, I never thought female empowerment was important to me. But I've been participating in a female empowerment program in recent months. What a coincidence! I think this is how synergy works.
- Perseverance: I need this right now. I know what I want to do, but sometimes I lose faith. To succeed, I have to have perseverance.

We are not always aware of our values. Exploring them and bringing them to the surface can facilitate our understanding of who we are. It can help us see the most essential things in our lives, the things that matter to us most.

What gives you your values?

Each of us has our own values. We were raised in different families, and each family has its own set of values. We read different books and watch different television programs. We've met different people and we've experienced life in our own ways. We follow different faiths. All of those factors make up a complex network of inner values. As you learned in chapter four, you don't own your thoughts. They are shaped by your external environment and culture you live in. Just the same, you do not necessarily own all of your values.

In traditional Chinese society, women tend to value a happy marriage. Because of its stress on happiness within marriage, Chinese society views a divorced woman in pejorative ways: she's been deserted and is unworthy of love. For men, the values of success and responsibility (in the sense that men shoulder the responsibility of providing for the family) predominate. In traditional Chinese popular culture, a good woman is kind, caring, loving, generous and tolerant. None of those values are associated with career and self-development.

If you ever get a chance to watch the Chinese television series *Empress in the Palace,* you'll understand the double standard. Based on historical fiction, *Empress in the Palace* has gained sweeping popularity in China and has attracted an international audience. It is about a young girl named Huan who overcomes her enemies and becomes a well-respected empress. Huan keeps her virtues of kindness, care, and tolerance, even for her enemies. Although *Empress in the Palace* is based on the palace life in the Yongzheng period of the Qing dynasty, its portrayal of traditional female virtues speaks to a modern audience.

But just as language changes, so do values. That's why you may find that the values your grandparents have are outdated. You might call it a generation gap. Young people in China don't necessarily embody our culture's traditional values. In certain segments of society, (for example, in higher education), independent females are celebrated.

Societies undergo their own stages of development. In the West, gender roles persist, but they tend to be more relaxed than they are in China. American society values success and wealth in both men and women. American films tend to depict women as caring and loving. But above all, women in American films are usually seeking self-fulfillment.

In the comedy series *This Is Us,* the lead female character Rebecca is dating a man from a privileged background. He has a decent job, and he is ready to marry her. But he doesn't support her passion for singing, so she leaves him. For a Chinese audience, that's hard to imagine, but the woman's decision would likely still elicit empathy.

In the television series *The Good Wife*, Alicia returns to her career in law after a public sex scandal erupts involving her husband. To Western audiences, the decision is natural. "We knew she had to go back to work," said Michelle King, one of the producers of the show.[123] In America, women feel less pressure to sacrifice their careers for the sake of their husband's.

As social animals, we can't help but be influenced by our culture. Its customs shape our own values. But can you identify values that reflect your true self, not those of your culture or society? You might argue with me, but if J.K. Rowling had grown up in Beijing, I think she would still be writing. If Henry Ford had grown up in Shanghai, he would still be acting. If Steve Jobs had grown up in Wuhan, he might not have founded Apple, but I bet he would have been an entrepreneur.

At some point, most of us find that some of our innermost values come into conflict with the values of the societies we live in. Perhaps those struggles, that negotiation of identity, is part of the human condition. If you were a woman living in Japan, you might struggle with the expectation that Japanese women give up their careers to take care of their children. What if you wanted to pursue your art career and be a good wife and mother at the same time? What would you do?

Staying true to yourself while following your innermost values is rarely the easiest choice.

Sometimes you may find that your values can change as you grow older, just as values in a society can evolve over time. When you were younger, your values might have been success and wealth. As you matured, you began to value peace and freedom. Or you might change the way you think about success and wealth. Regularly examining our value words enables you to see if they're in line with who we are.

Now my dear reader, if you're still struggling to get a handle on your innermost values and who you are at your core, don't fret. The following will help you gain some clarity.

Step Two: gain clarity about who you are and what you must do

When you've identified your value words, imagine yourself embodying them. Visualize yourself with the traits of someone who is peaceful, courageous, and strong—or whatever value words you've identified as admirable. In what ways are you acting in alignment with your core values?

If your values are peace and courage, what are you doing to demonstrate that you value peace and courage? What are you capable of achieving when you fully embody your core values? If you value joy and strength, what can you achieve when you are joyful and strong?

After sharing her story of Joan of Arc, my friend began applying her innermost values to her work. She decided to use her innermost values guide her through a writing project—a book about overcoming pain. She realized she could also rely on them to guide her public talks and to build online courses that help other people overcome physical pain and emotional trauma. Alleviating pain is something she realized she could do to serve others, enabling her to lead and influence people. To succeed, she would need the values of courage and perseverance to overcome her fears of not being good enough.

When my friend talked about aligning her work with her values, her excitement was palpable. I dug further: "Suppose your doctor told you that you only have three months to live. Which of those three activities do you feel you must do before you die?" She said the online program was the one thing that she must do. But if she had a year, she would do all three.

After that exercise, my friend communicated with absolute clarity what she wanted to do with her life. She laid out a path defined by who she truly is. Sometimes identifying who you are and what you *must* do requires you to change how you speak about your interests and passions. If your passion is teaching, and teaching defines who you are, rather than say that you want to teach, tell yourself you *must* teach. Say: "I *must* be a teacher." If you value service, environmental sustainability and nature, and they speak to who you are, you might decide you want to start a community garden. But don't say simply to yourself: "I want to start a community garden. Say: "I *must* start a community garden."

Before my friend spoke with me, she had a general idea about what she wanted to do with her life. But rephrasing those interests from "wants" to "musts" initiated an awakening for her. There may be many things in life you want to do, but there can only be a few things that you feel you must do. Those are the things that define you and make you *you*.

The expression "be what you must be" is more powerful and more motivating than "do what you want to do." Since "be what you must be" relates directly to your higher values of who you are, it activates your higher brain regions. Doing what you must do suggests you are fulfilling the highest level of human needs according to Maslow's hierarchy—self-actualization, which means achieving one's full potential. "Do what you want to do" could refer to any random desire in daily life, and those random desires often involve your lower brain functions.

When you achieve clarity around your values, you'll find it easier to arrive at an understanding of who you are and what you must become. If you have trouble identifying the most essential things in your life, try asking yourself: "What if I have only three months to live?" If that question doesn't deliver insights into what you must be, don't worry. Sometimes, it takes a particular experience to teach you what you must be. Sometimes that particular experience is failure. If you're unsure of what you must do or who you must become, simply remain awake to the question.

Take Walt Disney. In 1919, a newspaper editor fired him from his first job as a cartoonist. His boss told him that he was "lacking imagination" and had "no good ideas." Those words now seem ridiculous. Walt Disney went on to demonstrate his exemplary creative genius; he is still admired around the world for what he achieved. But those harsh words from an employer early on his career, along with his first job termination, enabled the cartoonist to realize that despite any criticism he might encounter in his career, a cartoonist is who he was. It was what he loved to do—what he *had to* do.

George Clooney also had to fail before he realized who he was and what he had to become. Clooney worked as a door-to-door insurance salesman and professional baseball player. He failed catastrophically at both. But those failures led him to discover his potential as an actor.

Sometimes we need setbacks, failures and frustrations to develop a firmer faith that we must do something or become somebody. If you are experiencing setbacks, failures, or frustrations right now, there is no better opportunity to investigate who you are and what you must become. When you achieve clarity about these two things, that clarity will grant you the determination to achieve anything you want in life. You will change from merely someone who has casual interests into someone who is committed to her passions and visions. Rather than merely wanting to do something or wanting to be somebody, you'll gain the tenacious ability to follow through with that one thing you must do, that one person you must become. Whoever that person is and whatever she ends up doing, she will honor and embody her deepest values in everything she does.

Step three: consider your value words every day and how they apply to every dimension of your life

Meditate briefly on your value words every morning. What is the value word that arises before you get out of bed? When you sit down to work toward your task for the day, what is the value word that guides you? Every night, when you evaluate your day and how you've spent your time—consider your values. Your values will keep you grounded. They'll help you maintain clarity about what you need to do. You'll feel happy when you know you are on track in realizing your values in everyday life. Research in neuroscience shows that thinking about your values releases 1,400 immune system boosters throughout your body!

You can apply similar tactics to elicit value words to guide you through other dimensions of your life, like your relationships and your business, if you have one. Or, you can simply ask yourself: *What kind of relationships make me happy? What kind of business do I want to create?* When you have established your values for those aspects of your life, think about them every time you are having an important conversation with your loved ones. Reflect on them before meeting your boss or launching a marketing campaign for your online business. The more you think about your values, the more you'll feel their power to help you achieve the results you desire. Value words are the most powerful and most important words around. Make the most of them.

In Summary

Knowing your values comes down to knowing who you truly are and what you have to do to live a life you desire. Such knowledge can act as a north star that navigates your ship through its darkest nights. Your value words are the most powerful in your life, yet it's not always easy to come up with them right away. Sometimes, it takes setbacks and failures to arrive at a sense of clarity of our values. This chapter provides you with a tool to help you elicit your value words, gain clarity, and live by your values.

Be aware that values are shaped by our external environment and the culture we live in, just like language. Staying true to yourself and following your values can face the most formidable challenge, as sometimes you may find your innermost values come into conflict with those of the societies we live in. Sometimes you may also find that your values change as you grow older, just as society's values can evolve over time.

Chapter 8: Transform the Story You Tell

"Narrative imagining—story—is the fundamental instrument of thought. Rational capacities depend on it. It is our chief means of looking into the future, of predicting, of planning, and of explaining…Most of our experience, our knowledge and our thinking is organized as stories."

Mark Turner[124]

We all tell stories and listen to stories. They draw the contours of our inner life and chart the customs of our social life. They contribute to our sense of who we are and what we might become.

Stories rely on language, so learning a new language gives you a chance to write new stories or reframe the old ones. A new language teaches you to adopt a new grammar and a fresh set of rules for being in the world. Once you take the opportunity to rewrite your story, you can reinvent yourself. Once you start playing with the generative role of language, anything is possible. You can reimagine the stories that have given shape and meaning to your life. You can add new chapters that will give you a new lease on life.

The stories you tell yourself make an impact on what's important to you. By changing the story, you can change your mindset. In this chapter, you'll learn how to reflect on your own stories as a starting point to gathering insight into your values, your sense of self, your obstacles, and your goals.

It can be challenging to see clearly how the stories we tell ourselves influence our day-to-day lives. But looking closely at those stories is the first step to writing a new one. Knowing your story in and out enables you to revise what you might have thought was set in stone. You learn that the story is malleable, and you can repurpose it. You might add a greater sense of freedom, joy, and clarity to the life of the main character. I call this a narrative approach. When you approach your life with narrative, you can steer the plotline with your own inner values.

Why stories?

Can you imagine life without stories?

My students love to hear stories. They might walk out at the end of class and forget everything they've learned, but they'll never forget a good story. If you scroll through Twitter, pick up a copy of *The New York Times*, or log onto Netflix—you'll see evidence that nearly everyone loves a good story. Stories live and breathe all around us. Some of those stories might inspire you. Some might distress you. A tweet about a doctor who saved a man's life but risked his own might inspire your inner hero. A story about a cop who shoots an unarmed black man tells another story, one that will likely distress you. But it also might inspire you to march with Black Lives Matter. The obituaries, the comics, the headlines—all are forms of storytelling. If a friend asks: "What happened to you last night?" no doubt, you'll end up telling that friend a story. If you're getting to know someone, you might compare notes on the stories of your lives. Stories are common to every culture. The act of listening to stories begins in infancy. Telling stories is how we organize information. Narratives give order to what otherwise might appear chaotic. We tell stories to make sense of the world, to make sense of ourselves.

For linguists, the act of storytelling is connected to the evolutionary development of language, or what linguists call the phylogenesis of language. It's similar to biological evolution. Michael Bamberg, a psychologist with a background in linguistics, has concentrated much of his research on the ways that humans use narrative to make sense of life, how they use it to form an identity. Bamberg suggests that stories are tied to our sense of individuality. He argues that our idea of the modern person comes from narrative (2012).[125]

Archeologists have seen evidence of the earliest narrative form—the epic—as far back as 1500 BCE. No one can say for certain when the earliest forms of language took shape. But forms of storytelling may have existed well before language.

Faculty director of Columbia University's seminar "Strategic Storytelling" Frank Rose is a self-proclaimed "digital anthropologist." He takes a special interest in how stories shape our reality. In *The Art of Immersion*, he writes, "Just as the brain detects patterns in the visual forms of nature—a face, a figure, a flower—and in sound, so too it detects patterns in information. Stories are recognizable patterns, and in those patterns, we find meaning."[126] Narrative, writes psychologist David Polkinghorne, is "the primary form by which human experience is made meaningful".[127] In *Man's Search for Meaning*, Viktor Frankl takes it further. To him, the human capacity to find meaning is a form of healing. It's not only language that differentiates human beings from other species, it's our relentless search for meaning, of healing, communicated through a story.[128]

Professor of Gerontology William Randall argues that we not only *have* a story, we *are* a story. In *The Stories We Live by: Personal Myths and the Making of the Self*, psychologist Dan McAdams agrees: "If I want to know myself, to gain insight into the meaning of my own life, then I, too, must come to know my own story."[129] McAdams calls that story our personal myth. We look to that myth to discover what is most important to us. "The universe," writes the American poet Muriel Rukeyser in her poem "The Speed of Darkness," "is made of stories, not of atoms."[130] Atoms may make up our materiality—but stories make up our sense of self.

As we discussed in chapter two, the culture you live in plays a significant role in determining what you find meaningful. Your background affects your sense of meaning, too. When you read an article in a magazine, you don't examine every word and every sentence. You take in what is meaningful to you, what appeals to you. Take this quote from Alex Altman's "Why the Killing of George Floyd Sparked an American Uprising" in the June 4th, 2020 issue of *Time:* "For 2½ months, America has been paralyzed by a plague, its streets eerily empty. Now pent-up energy and anxiety and rage have spilled out. COVID-19 laid bare the nation's broader racial inequities."[131]

What do you notice most in those two sentences? Which words catch your attention? Is it "plague," "pent-up," "anxiety," "rage," or "racial inequities"? Each word is provocative and evocative. But depending on your background, you might focus your attention on some words more than others. A person of color might notice the "racial inequities" and focus on how the pandemic has exacerbated those inequalities. A politician may see the word "rage" and consider how he'll respond to that rage in his campaign for election. A therapist may notice the words "pent-up" and "anxiety" and focus on all of the people who lack emotional support in a time of crisis.

Along those lines, when we talk to other people, we rarely listen fully and completely. We process their words through our own conscious and unconscious memories. We make personal and subjective connections to what they are saying. To make sense of speech, we refer to our own past impressions and experiences.

For instance, if I were to give all my students the same feedback on their work, each would respond in her own way. Some students would focus on the ways they can improve. Some would concentrate on what they did well. Others might fixate on the places they performed poorly. Some will inevitably catastrophize a low mark and consider it the end of the world. Students speak to me in their own ways. Some respond to feedback with trust and respect. Others doubt and challenge me. So much depends on their wiring: their memories and experiences, their lack or abundance of self-confidence and self-esteem, their sense of pride, their sense of failure, their fears and anxieties, their hopes and dreams.

To complicate matters further, we all have limits to how many words we can process at any one time. Your brain remembers only seven chunks of information at once. Referred to as "magical number seven" by psychologists when they discovered it in the 1950s, "seven chunks of information" illustrates the capacity of the working memory of our brain. If your long-term memory acts as a digital library, one that you can access at any moment (as long as you remember your password), working memory acts as a blackboard. You write things on it to help you manage a specific task. Then, you erase everything. When you hear someone speak, you use your working memory. You recollect 10 or 15 words that stand out for you. When you put those memorable words together, the result may differ from what the speaker had intended.

That explains why we often misunderstand each other. None of us has the capacity to comprehend the totality of what another person is saying. Our spouses, parents, and closest friends are, at heart, mysterious. And since we shape our inner lives in response from what we can take in from the world around us, it follows that we have a limited perception of ourselves, too. In the story of our own lives, we are all unreliable narrators.

Take for example the American television series *The Affair*, which premiered in 2014. Most episodes have two parts. One part is seen through the eyes of Noah, the man who is engaging in an extramarital affair with Alison, who is also married. The other through the point-of-view of Alison. It's interesting, but not surprising, to watch how differently Noah and Alison remember the same event. They each recall the events in their own sequence. The words and tone of conversations differ. They make their own omissions. They emphasize different emotions. Often, the memories of both stand in conflict to one another. One of the co-creators of *The Affair*, Sarah Treem, describes the show as "the *Rashomon* of relationship dramas."[132] *Rashomon* is a 1950 Japanese film that involves various characters who each offer alternative, self-serving and contradictory versions of the same incident. The term "Rashomon effect" refers to real-world situations where different eye-witnesses of an event present conflicting information.

Most characters—whether in fiction, film or real life—have only a partial, patchy perspective of the world. Leo Tolstoy's narrator in *Anna Karenina* is third-person omniscient, which means the narrator is "all-knowing." He slips in and out of the perspectives of dozens of characters. For two chapters, he even takes the perspective of a dog! "All-knowing," however, is a relative term. Even omniscient narrators are incomplete, and usually, at some level, unreliable.

Like Tolstoy's narrator in *Anna Karenina*, the narrator of James Joyce's *Ulysses* slips in and out of the consciousness of a collection of characters. The reader hears numerous voices throughout the narrative of single day—Thursday, June 16th—and a single city—Dublin, Ireland. To demonstrate how varied human perception of events can be, Joyce shifts from telling the story through newspaper headlines to internal monologues to first-person speculations.

In "stream-of-consciousness" forms of narration, you have access to everything that passes through a character's mind. But having access to someone's unfiltered thoughts and meandering impressions makes it all that much clearer how limited and subjective any one view of the world is. What's more, when discourses are at play with one another, they highlight how points-of-view can contradict, clash, or collaborate. As a reader, you can assess characters in the book based on multiple views and presentations. The same is true for your assessment of characters and events in the story of your life.

Like Joyce's characters in *Ulysses*, Tolstoy's characters in *Anna Karenina* or Ruth and Noah in Treem's *The Affair*, each of us sees the world—and ourselves—in our own ways. While culture, upbringing and education influence our stories, we all have our own personal narratives. Those tales we spin—coming-of-age stories, romances, and adventures—give a sense of cohesion, structure, and meaning to our lives. When we repeatedly tell those tales, we slowly take up residence in them. We eventually become them.

There is power in owning your story and living in the best version of it. But like any story, there's always the risk that it can own us. There's always a risk that the story we tell ourselves has little grounding in reality. In the framework of neuroscience, any version of reality is in some degree a fantasy, a hallucination. But it's easy to mistake the hallucination as reality.

Take F. Scott Fitzgerald's 1925 novel *The Great Gatsby*.[133] Raised on a farm in the Midwestern United States, the young Jay Gatsby dreams of achieving great wealth, success, and status. Convinced that an education is the ticket to all three, he enrolls in college. But his professors can't see his greatness, and

Gatsby grows disillusioned. Dropping out, he follows fortune by other means. He infiltrates aristocratic circles—first as an employee and then as a member of the nouveau riche. Rather than inherit wealth, Gatsby sells booze during a time of prohibition. He makes millions.

By nearly all accounts, Gatsby has realized the "American Dream." He's pulled himself out of poverty. He's fabulously wealthy. But when it comes to living by his innermost values, he remains impoverished. He mistakes the American Dream as his own. He pursues it by any means possible, even if it means obtaining wealth illegally. But what he longs for the most is love, in particular the love of a girl named Daisy, who is married to a Yale-educated millionaire.

It doesn't end well for Gatsby.

Even though Gatsby has realized a dream—one of fame and fortune—much of what he truly desires is never realized. Despite his wealth, he never feels wholly respected, admired, and loved by anyone.

But what if Gatsby had taken time to examine his story and his innermost values? Would his fate have been the same?

Erin Brockovich is the name of a popular movie from 2000 starring Julia Roberts. But it's also the name of a real life heroine, who, despite a lack of legal training, successfully built a law case against the Pacific Gas and Electric Company (PG&E) in 1993. Convinced that the rise in cancer cases in her community had come from contaminated drinking water, she fought against the multi-million dollar company responsible. Her involvement in the case led to a settlement of $133.6 million for her firm and a $2 million bonus for Brockovich.

Unlike the fictional Gatsby, the real-life Brockovich valued honesty and integrity and lived by those values. She believed in her own innate power to stand up to corporate misconduct. She believed in her community's right to safe drinking water. She put herself in the driver's seat and steered her case with a deep sense of altruism. She achieved fame and fortune but neither by selfish nor illegal means.

Whether we are rich or poor, many of us have grown comfortable in the stories we tell ourselves. Many people forget that their dreams, ambitions, and fears are nothing but stories. Most people forget that they are narrating those stories and they are far from omniscient or reliable. Human beings have a tendency to fill in the gaps and interpret events in ways that appeal to them. They omit critical details if it doesn't fit into their worldview. Many of the emotions any one of us experiences—like rage and fear—arise less in response to what is happening now and more in response to what has happened before. In many ways, everyone's experience of "reality" is a fantasy.

That's why it's important to not only ground your story in your innermost values but examine closely the stories you tell yourself. If the stories you're caught up in cause emotional distress, you can disrupt them. If your story of yourself is too far removed from the truth, you can learn to identify the lies and half-truths you are telling yourself that neither serve you nor the people around you. You can craft a new story. You can realign the new version with your deepest values. You can choose your own adventure.

But first you need to get a handle on the old myths you're living by.

Step one: Tell the old story

Writing vs. talking

Think about one thing that has been troubling you. Write it down. Or, talk about it to a friend whom you trust. Record your conservation. Listen to the recording. Transcribe the part that stands out for you. Or, do both.

As you speak or write, follow anything that comes to mind, spontaneously, without worrying where it might lead you. Don't set constraints around what you should say or write. Consider it a stream-of-consciousness activity. It'll help you gain access to your innermost thoughts and any unresolved feelings.

Whether you speak and write about whatever is troubling you, notice how the story changes slightly depending on the medium you use to tell it. Each form of storytelling offers hints of what you subconsciously believe to be true. The advantage of sharing your story aloud with a friend is that your friend can offer a fresh perspective. She can encourage you to reframe your story and stimulate your imagination to tell it a new way. The advantage of writing your story down is that it forces you to organize your thoughts and explore the problem deeply. Writing out your problem grants you a greater depth of perspective.

Step two: Get beneath the story.

When you finish writing or transcribing your story, read it as if you were an outsider looking in. Before you start reading, put yourself into a deeply relaxed state. Yawn deeply. Stretch slowly. Move as if you were in slow motion. Those preparatory activities interrupt the activities of your busy mind. They enable you to fully relax. You can softly touch the back of your hand, your palm, your fingers, or your face. Experiencing small, sensual pleasures can help your mind reach a state of relaxation.

When you feel deeply relaxed, read what you've written and ask yourself the following questions.

1. What words or phrases catch my attention?
2. How do they make me feel?
3. What is my story beneath my choice of words?

Below is an excerpt from a conversation I had with one of my American friends. We did this exercise together. When I asked her to share something that was troubling her, she began talking about her fears around the coronavirus. Read the excerpt below and consider the questions: What words stick out for you? How do those words make you feel? What do you think is the story, or the set of beliefs, beneath the words?

When something big happens, we tend to think of our own survival first. Because of my age, and because I have been so sick for so long (with an illness that affects my lungs), I'm vulnerable. I'm in a high-risk category. Statistically, I am in the ten percent of people most vulnerable to infection. There's people in that ten percent with diabetes or heart disease. I don't have those things. I'm better off than that ten percent of people. But I know what it is like to be sick. I've been working hard to keep myself safe. The thing that distresses me is that you have to sanitize everything that comes into the house. I think people are making more of an effort to stay home. But people are still going out. Every time I touch plastic, I have to dispose of the plastic, and I have to wash my hands. Part of me is asking: "How can I not make a mistake?"

What words or phrases catch your attention?

Perhaps "survival," "die," "ten percent," "distress," "working hard," or "mistake" stick out for you.

How do those words make you feel?

The words "survival" and "die" might arouse feelings of fear. The word "distress" might bring up pain or panic. The narrator tells us that she is "working hard," but her hard work is not pleasurable to her. It's exhausting and overwhelming to have to sanitize everything. The word "mistake" suggests feelings of shame. It implies the narrator blames herself for not doing enough.

So, what is happening beneath the surface of her speech? What is going on for my friend at a subconscious level?

Let's go through the story once again. Pay close attention to the underlined phrases. Notice if they trigger anything for you.

When something big (1) happens, we tend to think of our own survival (2) first. Because of my age (3) and because I have been so sick for so long (with an illness that affects my lungs), (5) I'm vulnerable (6). I'm in a high-risk category (7). Statistically, I am in the ten percent of people most vulnerable to infection (8). There's people in that ten percent with diabetes or heart diseases. I don't have those things. I'm better off (9) than that ten percent. But I know what it is like to be sick (10). I've been working hard to beat it (11). The thing that distresses me (12) is that you have to (13) sanitize everything that comes into the house. I think people are making more of an effort to stay home, but people are still going out (14). Every time I touch plastic, I have to (13) dispose of the plastic, and I have to (13) wash my hands. Part of me is asking (15): "How can I not make a mistake?" (16)

Examine the underlined parts. Can you read between the lines? Read the words intuitively and empathize with the feelings behind them.

1. big: This is having a big impact on my life.
2. our own survival: I feel threatened.
3. my age: I'm old.
4. I have been so sick for so long: My sickness makes me vulnerable.
5. affects my lungs: My lungs are not in the best condition.
6. I'm vulnerable to infection: I'm in a bad situation.
7. I'm in a high-risk category: It's likely I might die if I catch the virus.
8. the ten percent: The possibility is high.
9. I'm a little better off: I'm slightly better off, but I'm still at a high risk.
10. what it is like to be sick: Being sick is a horrible experience.
11. I've been working hard to beat it: I'm making an effort to protect myself, but who knows?
12. distresses me: I'm in pain.
13. have to (repeated three times): I don't have a choice. I'm forced to do this.
14. people are still going out: The situation is out of control.
15. Part of me is asking: This is always in the back of my mind.
16. How can I not make a mistake: It's likely that I make a mistake.

Are you beginning to see the story beneath the story?

When you do this exercise, keep a first-person perspective. For me, the story beneath my friend's story goes like this.

> The pandemic is killing people. I'm old, and I'm sick. One of my lungs is weak. If I catch the coronavirus, I might die. I have neither diabetes nor heart disease, but I still might die from this. It's horrible to be sick. I've been working hard to take protective measures. But the results will be the same regardless of what I do. Sanitizing everything and washing my hands every time I touch plastic is distressing and painful. There are still people going out, spreading the contagion. The whole thing is out of my control.

Your version of my friend's story might not be exactly the same, but I imagine it's similar. Underneath it all, the narrator feels afraid and out of control.

Now let's have a closer look at the unresolved, subconscious beliefs that might be underpinning the story. It's not difficult to arrive at the following:

1. I will always be in poor health.
2. I'm not doing enough. I will make a mistake.

Since my friend has been affected by a long-term illness, she has developed the outlook that she will always be in poor health. But when I elicited more information from her, she told me that her doctor had told her that she has a strong immune system—a fact my friend had nearly forgotten. The doctor's words didn't fit into the story my friend had been telling herself.

When analyzing stories, focus on what the narrator is saying. But also pay attention to what's not said, the unspoken story beneath the words and the language expressed through the body.

My friend's belief about her own poor health is so deep-seated that she ignored her own doctor. We tend to listen to words that speak to our beliefs.

For those that don't, we turn a blind eye. In *The Great Gatsby*, Gatsby invents his own story. He's "Great" because he's great at telling himself a story. He believes his story so much that he'll do anything to make it come true. He grows fabulously wealthy. But he also deludes himself. He doesn't understand his story. He doesn't know the story beneath the story. He doesn't know what he deeply values. On the surface, he's succeeded. But behind his own lies, he's failed miserably.

Gatsby's story is extreme. But we all delude ourselves. We all convince ourselves that the world is something other than it is. We tell ourselves we are not good enough as we are, that we are never doing enough. For that reason, you may find the narrator's second belief familiar. How many times have you hesitated going forward in your life because you've feared making a mistake? Many of us live with the belief that we are incomplete, that we are not enough. If this sounds familiar, it's not your fault. Often our ideas of what is "good enough" come from the ways we were raised or taught, our memories and the standards we live by.

For a child who grows up with a mother with unattainable standards, he may find that adulthood that he feels he's never enough. If his mother never praised him, never approved of him—or was overly critical—that child may seek praise or approval in ways that are unhealthy and a threat to his own well-being.

A young woman who partners up with a man who doesn't value her opinions, recognize her talents or honor her time may develop a belief that her opinions, qualities and time are not worth much. She may eventually fall into the trap of thinking that she is somehow unworthy. She may grow depressed if she internalizes those beliefs.

As much as we like to think we'd be better off if we grew up with a mother who always praised us or a partner who appreciated us all of the time, it's a fantasy. None of us will ever live in an ideal world. None of us grow up in a 100 percent affirmative environment with parents, peers, and partners that never fail to encourage and support us. As we go through life, it is impossible to avoid negative comments, neglect, or criticism.

Besides, if we had grown up with endless praise by our parents and peers, we would likely develop other issues. We've all had conflicts in our pasts, if not traumas. Those shore up in the stories we tell, too.

But is it possible to interrupt those stories if they are harming you? Can you repurpose them? A story told in a new way can lift you up, just as the old ones can put you down.

Step three: Write a new story.

You cannot change what has already happened to you. But you can change how you interpret the events that have happened to you. You can edit the story you tell yourself, or from it, you can write a new one.

Of course, there are facts in every story that need to be there. You cannot change the fact that the pandemic has happened, that the virus is contagious, and that anyone can get COVID-19 from an unknown source. The virus kills people. That's undeniable. It's something that my friend needs to acknowledge when she rewrites her story. For Gatsby, he knew that he was hiding the source of his wealth, but he convinced himself that extreme wealth was the only measure of his worth. Concealing the truth led to his tragic ending.

To take my friend's story as an example, most stories are filled with uncertainties. She fears the spread of the coronavirus and believes that it will kill her. Neither her fears nor her beliefs are based on facts and reality, but the brain has difficulty determining one from the other. It reacts as if her fears were real.

Plus, the brain has a negativity bias. It tends to focus on any possible negative outcome of uncertain situations. From an evolutionary standpoint, the brain uses that bias to guard against potential risk and danger. That's why the word "uncertainty" itself is unsettling and can trigger unpleasant emotions.

But what if we change the word "uncertainty" to "not knowing?" How does that make you feel? "Not knowing" points to something unknown, mysterious. It might mean that something we desire awaits us. That triggers positive emotions. Changing a single word or phrase can turn any story around. Here's a rewrite of my friend's story.

There is a pandemic happening right now. I do not know the outcome. But I will stay as healthy and peaceful as I possibly can. I have a strong immune system, which is a blessing for someone at my age. I have experienced illness. I know what to do to protect myself. It's easy for me to take those protective measures. I will be safe and secure. When faced with a situation like this, my mental health matters. I know I have a strong mind, and that will help me build a strong body.

How does reading the second version feel to you? Do you find it uplifting? In contrast to the first version, the narrator communicates a sense of taking charge. She's proactive. In the first version of the story, she sits in the passenger seat of her own experience. In the revised version, she's sitting in the driver's seat. In the first version, the pandemic is controlling her, forcing her to do things. In the second version, she's in control, choosing to do things.

If my friend were Chinese. I would rewrite her story in Chinese. When translated back into English, it might appear like this:

> The pandemic is out there. No one knows how it will unfold. But the universe will run its own course. It will go away when the time comes. Before that time, I will do my best to take protective measures. As long as I make my best effort, things will just be fine. While I'm old, I still have a good immune system, which I regard as lucky. Though I've experienced long-term illness, I've not been defeated by any disease. I have a strong body and a strong mind.

In this version, I've integrated a Chinese philosophy of living into the translation. The idea that the universe has its own course is rooted in into

Chinese culture. The idea that if individuals do their best, they will reap the best results is integrated into daily life. But in both the English and Chinese revisions, the narrator takes charge and is at the helm of her experience. When you write a new story, remember that you are the narrator, that you are in control. Instead of playing a supporting role in your own life, take center stage. You are the hero.

My revisions of my friend's original story are just two possibilities among many. Write your own updated version. Be playful with words. Use your imagination. Every one of us can be creative. Imagine your role model or someone you admire in your life. Consider what that person might do in your situation. Feel empowered when you rewrite your story.

Also, use short, simple sentences. Write concisely. Your brain will more easily digest the information that way. Remember that your brain can only process seven units of meaning at a time. If you write a short story, there's less of a chance that your brain will misinterpret the words. If the story is too long, there's a greater opportunity for multiple interpretations. Focus on the key messages.

What if your old story keeps popping up? Some neuro tips to put it down quickly.

When you've written your new story, practice it. Tell it to yourself as much as possible. Write it down. Record it. Ritually play it or read it daily. Listen to it anytime you feel down. The more you practice it, the better the chances that your mind will believe it. Just as it takes time to develop a muscle, it takes time to develop new habits and new beliefs.

Be aware that your old stories and new stories will co-exist. But now you have the choice of which version runs the show. Don't underestimate how powerful our old story is. It has developed roots in your subconsciousness. Some of your beliefs can be so deeply rooted that your brain will do everything to protect them. You protect your old stories often without any awareness that you are doing it.

It's inevitable that your old stories will pop up, so don't take that as a sign of failure. You might find the pain triggered by those old stories overwhelming. You might feel stuck in the old stories and find it too difficult to pull yourself out of the tangle. But there are exercises you can do to train your brain to release the grip of old beliefs. Neuro tips—or strategies based on studies in neuroscience—can help you let go of old, distressing stories. Your brain can interrupt any strong emotions triggered by them.

First, take a slow stretch and yawn deeply. We talked about the benefit of doing this in chapter three. Relaxing stops the busy clatter in your head and enables you to shift your state of mind in as fast as a few seconds.

After you yawn, move your body as if you were in a slow-motion scene in a movie. Moving your body slowly directs you to an experiential consciousness of the environment and of your own body. Roll your neck as slowly as possible, so slowly that it takes about one or two minutes to finish a complete rotation.

All of those small, simple actions will guide you into a deeply relaxed state. They will help ground you in the present, which diverts you from rumination.

Second, observe any past memories that unfold in your story without judgment, just like an outsider. Recall the memory of your story inch by inch, bit by bit, from the beginning to the end. Immerse yourself fully in the feeling and experience of your story. Stay deeply relaxed. If you find yourself getting tense, repeat the steps in the first tip. In a relaxed state, it is easier to position yourself as an outsider to your own story. That will help you distance yourself from the pain of reexperiencing it.

Third, engage in pleasant self-nurturing. If when you observe your old story you feel pain, gently stroke your own hand. Touch your palm, your fingers or your face. Grab a soft pillow, blanket, or plush toy and hug yourself with it in your arms. Do whatever is most comfortable and pleasurable to you. For most people, gently stroking their skin or hugging a pillow interrupts any strong negative emotions that accompany painful memories. But if those strategies fail or if your body rejects them, stop. It might be a sign of childhood abuse, and you're best to turn to professional help to guide you further.

The theory behind all of these strategies is memory reconsolidation. When painful memories of your story arise, you can meet them in a relaxed way. That will alter their effect on you. You're embedding sensations of relaxation and pleasure into the memory circuit of the old story. That will reduce the neurological pain associated with the memory.

All those strategies can be called by another name—mindfulness, as mentioned in earlier chapters. "Mindfulness" means moment-to-moment nonjudgmental awareness of thoughts, feelings, sensations, and memories. As memories arise, stay mindful and nonjudgmental of them. Stay relaxed.

Most of us are unaware of how our emotions drive our thoughts and behaviors. We're often caught in the past or the future. We're rarely completely present for what's happening right now. Instead, we get trapped in fantasies. Those fantasies shape the structure and function of our brains. By practicing mindfulness, you can train the mind to let go of fixation on stories about the past and the future, thus releasing any pain associated with them.

The ability to experience the present fully helps us to live fully. As we discussed in previous chapters, Panksepp demonstrates how the mind is primarily driven by emotions. Most of the time, you're not conscious of passing experiences unless you associate strong feelings or sensations with them. That explains why you tend to forget most things that happen to you throughout the day.

Can you remember what you ate for lunch three days ago? Unless something memorable happened with that meal, you've likely already forgotten it. But if you experienced a strong emotion or sensation—whether positive or negative—when eating lunch three days ago, you'll store it in your memory.

In that sense, human consciousness is limited. But you can use mindfulness strategies to expand your consciousness, develop deeper awareness and get in touch with the emotions that are happening in the present moment, even if they don't evoke deep emotions. That allows you to simply see more and feel more. It also helps you gain a perspective of life that's not constrained by your emotions.

When you develop mindful awareness and a capacity to stay present, you can also open the doors to your creativity. Everyone can be imaginative. But if you get caught up in daily chatter, you'll lose the opportunity to tap into the greater potential of your mind and heart.

In Summary

It is our nature to need stories and tell stories. Stories make us human. They are tied to our sense of individualities and shape our identities. We tell our stories using our particular lens to perceive the world and ourselves, and there's always a risk that they have little grounding in reality. Likewise, we turn to our frames of interpretation to make sense of others' stories—in a way that appeals to our past impressions and experiences. But you can always reimagine the stories that have given shape and meaning and meaning to your lives. You can take charge of your own narrative and be at the helm of your life. By changing the story, you change the way you experience reality; you change your mindset; and you add new chapters that will give you a new lease on life. In this chapter, I provided you an action guide for you to achieve all of these. It helps you:

- Get a handle on the story you are telling yourself and gather insights into your values, sense of self, obstacles, and goals.
- Write a new story that frees you from the chains of your subconscious mind and empowers you to take charge and become the leading character of your own life.

Be aware that your old story will coexist with your new story for a very long time. You have to practice the new story long enough to rewire your brain and imprint that new story into your mind and everyday life. If the old story pops up, apply the neurotips at the end of the chapter. They will help you release the grip of the old stories in the fastest way ever possible. Try them. You'll be surprised.

Chapter 9: Get Motivation, Action and Manifest the Life You Desire

When you have achieved clarity about who you must become and what you must do, ask yourself what stops you from becoming who you are and manifesting the life you desire. You might think: "I'm not good enough," "I don't have enough knowledge," or "I'm afraid of failure." Obstacles to success usually fall under three categories: 1) mindset, 2) knowledge, and 3) skills. You may find yourself up against your own negative thinking, a lack of knowledge or a deficient skills-set. But all of those obstacles can be overcome.

When you say that you aren't good enough for what you feel you do, or that you are afraid of failure, it's your own mindset undermining you. Your mindset can stop you from living your best life. A negative mindset is usually connected with a negative story that you tell yourself about yourself. If you're telling yourself a negative story and saying to yourself that you are not good enough, return to the previous chapter. Use the action guide and neuro tips to create a new story that embraces a positive mindset.

Once you've achieved clarity and a positive mindset, you win half the battle. But the other half is still important. You need to get motivation and action right now. You need to start making plans right now. I am not talking about making resolutions, like you do on New Year's Eve. I am talking about making plans that lead to results. For that, you need a system. You need a method that ensures you can make the kind of plans that enable you to achieve your goals.

Step one: create your vision board.

Known as dream boards, your vision board represents the ideal life you want. It's a tool for you to visualize yourself, having achieved what you want with your life. Visualization stimulates positive emotions and encourages your brain to release dopamine.[134] Furthermore, a fantasy of the future helps you see and feel the rewards you'll get when you engage in certain behaviors. That also helps activate the SEEKING system, which then encourages the brain to release more dopamine. When your brain associates a reward with the activities you do to meet your goals, your SEEKING system will activate. That will keep you motivated.

If you have clarity about who you are and what you must do, it's important to illustrate it visually. Here are what you can do to make an empowering vision board:

First, visualize a scene where you have become who you truly are and lead the life you desire. Where are you? What are you doing? How do you look? How do you feel?

Second, when you know what your ideal life looks like, think about what you need to accomplish to live a life like that. Write down your most important goals in the next year.

Third, add your values words and motivational words that represent how you want to feel. Examples can be "powerful," "invincible," "unstoppable," "confident," "joyful," etc.

Fourth, find pictures and images representing your goals and dream life and that speaks to you. You can find them in magazines, the internet, or any place in your life—like a poster on the street. You can also add one of your favorite photos to this collection.

Now it's time to make your vision board. Get yourself a poster paper and start crafting it using what you have on the above. Enjoy the process. Get creative.

When you have your vision board ready, place it somewhere you can see easily every day. Take a few minutes to look it over at least once or twice a day. You can do this in the morning and/or every night before you go to bed. That way, it will ground your subconscious mind in line with your goals and values. As Jack Canfield said, "Your brain will work tirelessly to achieve the statements you give your subconscious mind. And when those statements are the affirmations and images of your goals, you are determined to achieve them!"[135]

Step two: design a process of realizing your visions.

When you have your goals and vision board at your hand, you need a process that translates them into reality, one that doesn't fail. You might ask, how can you make sure your process doesn't fail? Yes, you can. But first, you need to do enough homework. If you want to build an online business, look for those who have already done what you want to do. How did they do it? What are the mistakes you should avoid? Are there any proven models or methods that will lead you toward success? You might say there are business secrets people would prefer not to tell. Check what the most successful in your area have written and spoken. Read as much as you can. Learn as much as you can.

When you have done thorough research following the above mentioned, it won't be difficult for you to design your own process in which you divide your big goal into small ones for different stages and time periods. You should then set objectives and key results for each small goal. That's how you design your process and make plans. When you follow clear steps laid out clearly in the process you design, you'll surely reach your goal sooner or later. It's just a matter of time. If your process is sound, the outcome takes care of itself.

For example, if your overall plan is to start an online business, break the work into smaller chunks, and follow the process you've designed to finish the work for each chunk. Your online business might require you to design and develop products, build customers and generate leads, create an online platform and a mailing list, run marketing campaigns, get feedback on what you've done, and iterate accordingly. Make a timeline for working on each of these chunks and set deadlines for completing each.

When you start your action plan, make sure your daily targets are easy and simple to follow. For example, if you want to become a writer, start writing

100 words per day. You might think that doesn't make sense. If you want to commit to writing, why would you invest so little time to begin with? But investing a little time at the outset is how willpower gathers steam. If you start with writing 1,000 words or more a day, you might be able to meet your target at the beginning. But it may be difficult to maintain that daily quota of 1,000 words. Distractions will inevitably slow you down. You may find that you have less time in the day than you'd imagined. You could suffer from writers' block. When you fail to meet your target, you'll grow frustrated, lose motivation, and feel disempowered. You'll lose your energy. That will affect your ability to sustain your enthusiasm for your writing.

But if you plan to reach a more manageable target of 100 words, it's an entirely different story. First, writing 100 words does not take much will power. It is easy to follow that plan. You may find yourself writing more than 100 words. Of course, there may be times when you do not feel like writing at all. But by keeping the target at 100 words, you'll develop a habit. You'll develop consistency and perseverance. When writing 100 words per day becomes as natural as eating or breathing, you can set more ambitious targets. Once that happens, it will only be a matter of time before you achieve your writing goals.

Step three: track your progress and how you spend your time.

How well you carry out your plan depends on how well you spend your time. Simple, right? We all know that time is precious, yet we all find ourselves wasting it. If you want to develop efficiency in achieving your goals, value your time the same way you value your life. The way you spend your minutes, hours ,and days determines how you spend your life. You have to invest your time wisely.

Just as you created a system to manage your time to more efficiently reach your goals, create a system that enables you to check consistently how you spend your time and what progress you're making. The following questions will help you gain clarity around how you use your time.

- What did you do today? How long did it take?
- What were the things you did that contributed to you achieving your goal? What progress did you make? What were the things that you did that did not directly contribute to achieving your goal?
- How can you improve the way you spend your time tomorrow?

If you consistently evaluate how you spend your time and consider the progress you are making toward your overall goal each day, you will develop a greater sense of awareness of how you use your time. You'll be able to identify anything you do that does not contribute to achieving your goal. You will learn to say "no" to things and people that fail to nurture you. You'll put aside anything that consumes too much of you emotionally. You will learn to focus on the most essential things in your life, those things that support you to become who you are.

Be aware that slip ups happen. If you have one or two (or even more) days when you are not on track, find a way to forgive yourself. No one can stay on track every day of every week of every month. The ability to forgive yourself and manage your slip ups enables you to recover quickly. If you feel frustrated for not accomplishing as much as you would have liked to, forgive yourself. That will help you to create momentum over the long term. As a Chinese saying goes: "Get onto your feet as soon as possible when you stumble." We all stumble at some stage in our lives, but not everybody can get back onto their feet quickly. Self-forgiveness helps you get back on your feet.

Some neuro tips to boost your energy

Whether you like it or not, your energy levels, like everyone's, undergo cycles of highs and lows. There will be good days when you can achieve more than you expect. There will be bad days when you lack motivation. It happens. Luckily, there are strategies you can follow to enable your brain to function optimally most, if not all, of the time. These strategies will help you feel motivated and filled with energy.

First, use affirmation statements daily. Start every morning with affirmation statements. It helps if you've already written down general affirmation statements that you can use and tweak at will. For example, if you want to write a book, begin each day by affirming: "There's an author in me. I have all the discipline I need to finish this book. I am extremely creative. I create great work." You can also write down new affirmation statements for specific situations, like the COVID-19 pandemic. You might use affirmative statements like: "I have a strong immune system"; "I feel safe and secure"; "A healthy mind matters more than a healthy body"; "I am stronger than anything that comes in my way"; and "Nothing beats me except myself." Again, those are just examples. Feel free to work on your own. Use affirmation statements that speak to you and elevate you.

Pay attention that when you are making affirmative statements that you are using the present tense. That will enable your brain to believe that you are talking about facts. When your brain believes all the positive things you are saying to yourself, it stimulates your positive emotions and your brain lights up, enabling you to be consciously aware. It helps activate the SEEKING system and gives you the motivation to do the things that you want to do.[136]

Second, revisit the neurotips I gave in chapter six. Though they are designed to help you pump up your learning, they will achieve the same benefit for you to boost your productivity, as they help you tap your brain's hidden potential in the most efficient way. You'll have easy access to your intuition and creativity; you have a healthier brain anchored in a positive state of mind in peace and happiness.

In Summary

Half the battle to manifest the life you desire is achieving clarity about who you are and what you must do (a focus for chapter seven) and having the right mindset (a focus for chapter eight). But the other half is still desperately important. You need to get motivation and action! Without them, you can only live your ideal life in your dream. In this chapter, I provided you an action guide for you to:

- create a vision board to stay motivated.
- design a process that doesn't fail and make plans that leads to results.
- track your progress and increase productivity.
- use neurotips to boost your energy.

A Last Word

I've seen so many students/clients who came to me, saying, "Anna, I got so inspired and motivated every time we had a class/session, but my motivation fades quickly afterward." The difference between knowing what to do and doing it is heaven and hell. It explains essentially why some make changes happen, while others wait till they can not stand the suffering anymore.

My dear reader, now you've had a deeper understanding of the sheer power of language in defining and altering lives. I hope this does not happen to you. And it doesn't have to be. Here's how to keep your head up when you are down.

Start to talk to yourself using the language, "I must do this (or I must change)," "I'm capable of doing anything (or become anyone) if I decide to do it (or to be that person)." Stop using statements like "I'll try this or that," "It's not the end of the world if I don't do this or become that person," which reveals a testing attitude rather than a firm commitment. If you are swaying, you make excuses. If you are committed, you make it happen.

Experiment with the tips and techniques presented throughout this book. You can fine-tune them to fit your personal style and situations. Stay open-minded for any idea that does not appeal to you at first. Have an open heart for changes. Embrace them, with the assurance that you now have new tools and guides to help you replace old mindsets and habits that limit you from achieving the new life you desire. Avoid statements like "I'll try this tomorrow" or "I'm too busy now." The chances are that you may never get to it. Try it right now. Appreciate the changes it brings to you, knowing there's more to come. If you can not see the changes right now, give it time and patience. While some strategies, like yawning and slow movements, usually bring immediate benefits, others, like applying core values in all areas of your life, take time to be seeded in your brain. Don't jump to the conclusion "this is not working" too quickly. Such defeatist statements mean you've failed to find a way to get away from your old mindset—one usually comes with anxiety, fear, and discomfort, which will let you slip back into your old life, and your problem remains unsolved. In contrast, statements like "how can I make this work" reflect the commitment and a "can do" attitude, which will drive you toward success.

I hope you'll use the tools and guides to unlock the power of the language to change your life. I hope you get in touch with your deepest inner values, desires, motivation, and the genius in you and that you gain clarity in life and a sense of meaning and purpose. With a profound understanding of what language can do for you, look forward to having a positive attitude toward your new life, peace, happiness, and a new identity of yourself.

Acknowledgments

In and of itself, this book is driven by my own journey with language—a story of life, struggle, and transformation. But in large part, it is based on my learning from my teacher, neuroscientist (groundbreaker in the study of mindfulness and brain network theory and the application of the two in therapy), and neurocoach trainer Mark Robert Waldman. He opened up a new world for me, guided me to become a neurocoach and bring changes to the world, and inspired me to study the intriguing topic of language, mind, and the brain. Without your support and guidance, this book would have never come into existence.

I wish to acknowledge my students' and clients' contributions, who had discussions with me about what language is for them, and shared their difficulties and triumphs in life—those courageous individuals who dare to desire changes and seek help.

I would like to thank my mom, dad and younger brother for their constant love and support. I'm grateful that I have an angle in life—my son Marco, who has always been an inspiration and motivation for me to aim high and become the best I can be. My friends and colleagues deserve special mention for their support over the years. I want to thank my friend Elizabeth Kabanyan, Rei McColley, and Suzy Christensen for the ignited discussions we had, and my colleagues at Beijing Normal University for their support and help, especially Professor Xiaotang Cheng, who read my draft, Professor Shaoqian Luo, Professor Guangzhou Wang, and Professor Fuan Liu. Special thanks is extended to Professor Rob Tierney, Professor David Turner, and my supervisor John O'Regan, who read through drafts and offered insights and constructive criticism.

My most profound appreciation goes to my editors for their excellent editing skills and valuable feedback. I'm grateful for Nancy Miller, who helped me with my early drafts. She made my ideas shine while achieving clarity. She offered useful suggestions and commented on entertaining and informing a general audience. I especially wish to acknowledge the support, inspiration, and wise counsel I got from Surbhi Sanchali and her team, who had been there throughout as a friend and was ready to help anytime. Both of them contributed significantly to this book.

Notes

[1] Okrent, Arika. *In the land of invented languages: Esperanto rock stars, Klingon poets, Loglan lovers, and the mad dreamers who tried to build a perfect language.* Spiegel & Grau, 2009.

[2] *Ch'uan Teng Lu,* 22, quoted in Alan Watts' *The Way of Zen,* New York, Pantheon Books, 1951.

[3] Helene Cixous. AZQuotes.com, Wind and Fly LTD, 2020. https://www.azquotes.com/quote/1170379, accessed November 15, 2020.

[4] Julia Penelope. AZQuotes.com, Wind and Fly LTD, 2020. https://www.azquotes.com/quote/1160042, accessed November 15, 2020.

[5] Ralph Waldo Emerson. AZQuotes.com, Wind and Fly LTD, 2020. https://www.azquotes.com/quote/517963, accessed November 15, 2020.

[6] Rudyard Kipling. AZQuotes.com, Wind and Fly LTD, 2020. https://www.azquotes.com/quote/159915, accessed November 15, 2020

[7] Panksepp, Jaak, and Lucy Biven. *The archaeology of mind: neuroevolutionary origins of human emotions (Norton series on interpersonal neurobiology).* WW Norton & Company, 2012.

[8] Adrienne Rich. AZQuotes.com, Wind and Fly LTD, 2020. https://www.azquotes.com/quote/244191, accessed November 15, 2020.

[9] Smith, Frank. *To think: In language, learning and education.* Routledge, 2014.

[10] Geoffrey Willans Quotes. Goodreads.com. 2020

https://www.goodreads.com/quotes/9719229-you-can-never-understand-one-language-until-you-understand-at, accessed July 11, 2020.

[11] Goethe, Johann. *Maxims and reflections.* Penguin UK, 1998.

[12] Albert Einstein Quotes. BrainyQuote.com, BrainyMedia Inc, 2020. https://www.brainyquote.com/quotes/albert_einstein_108304, accessed July 11, 2020.

[13] Federico Fellini Quotes. BrainyQuote.com, BrainyMedia Inc, 2020. https://www.brainyquote.com/quotes/federico_fellini_106347, accessed July 11, 2020.

[14] Chesterton, Gilbert Keith. *What I saw in America.* Anthem Press, 2009.

[15] Panksepp, Jaak, and Lucy Biven. *The archaeology of mind: neuroevolutionary origins of human emotions (Norton series on interpersonal neurobiology).* WW Norton & Company, 2012.

Wright, Jason S., and Jaak Panksepp. "An evolutionary framework to understand foraging, wanting, and desire: the neuropsychology of the SEEKING system." *Neuropsychoanalysis* 14, no. 1 (2012): 5-39.

[16] Fox, Kate. *Watching the English: the hidden rules of English behavior revised and updated.* Nicholas Brealey, 2014.

[17] Jones, Barry. *Exploring otherness: An approach to cultural awareness.* London: CILT, 1995.

[18] Csikszentmihalyi, Mihaly, and Mihaly Csikzentmihaly. *Flow: The psychology of optimal experience.* Vol. 1990. New York: Harper & Row, 1990.

[19] Derrida, Jacques. *Monolingualism of the Other, or, the Prosthesis of Origin.* Stanford University Press, 1998.

[20] Desmond Tutu Quotes. Goodread.com. 2020

https://www.goodreads.com/quotes/141429-language-is-very-powerful-language-does-not-just-describe-reality. accessed July 11, 2020

[21] Wittgenstein, Ludwig. "Tractatus Logico-Philosophicus (trans. Pears and McGuinness)." (1961).

[22] Ethnologue: languages of the world. Ethnologue.com.

https://www.ethnologue.com, accessed March 2020.

[23] Majid, Asifa, and Niclas Burenhult. "Odors are expressible in language, as long as you speak the right language." Cognition130, no. 2 (2014): 266-270.

[24] Luhrmann, T. M. "Can't place that smell? You must be American." The New York Times 5 (2014).

[25] Boroditsky, Lera. "How does our language shape the way we think." What's next (2009): 116-129.

[26] Pennycook, Alastair. Language as a local practice. Routledge, 2010.

[27] Fei, Xiaotong. "Peasant life in China: a field study of country life inthe Yangtze valley." London: Kegan Paul. FeiPeasant Life in China: a Field Study of Country Life in the Yangtze Valley1939 (1939).

[28] Oliver Wendell Holmes, Sr. Quotes. BrainyQuote.com, BrainyMedia Inc, 2020. https://www.brainyquote.com/quotes/oliver_wendell_holmes_sr_152697, accessed November 25, 2020.

[29] Keane, Fergal. Letter to Daniel: despatches from the heart. London: Penguin, 1996.

[30] Chen, M. Keith. "The effect of language on economic behavior: Evidence from savings rates, health behaviors, and retirement assets." American Economic Review 103, no. 2 (2013): 690-731.

[31] Lamm, Bettina, Heidi Keller, Johanna Teiser, Helene Gudi, Relindis D. Yovsi, Claudia Freitag, Sonja Poloczek et al. "Waiting for the second treat: Developing culture-specific modes of self-regulation." Child Development 89, no. 3 (2018): e261-e277.

[32] Top Performing countries. NCEE.org. National Center on Education and Economy. 2020

https://ncee.org/what-we-do/center-on-international-education-benchmarking/top-performing-countries/. accessed July 2020.

[33] Chu, Lenora. Little soldiers: An American boy, a Chinese school and the global race to achieve. Hachette UK, 2017.

[34] Griffiths, Jay. *A sideways look at time*. Penguin, 2004.

[35] Lacan, Jacques, Alan Sheridan, and Malcolm Bowie. "The function and field of speech and language in psychoanalysis." In *Écrits: A selection*, pp. 33-125. Routledge, 2020.

[36] Wittgenstein, Ludwig. "Tractatus Logico-Philosophicus (trans. Pears and McGuinness)." (1961).

[37]Massen, Jorg JM, Kim Dusch, Omar Tonsi Eldakar, and Andrew C. Gallup. "A thermal window for yawning in humans: yawning as a brain cooling mechanism." *Physiology & Behavior* 130 (2014): 145-148.

Romero, Teresa, Marie Ito, Atsuko Saito, and Toshikazu Hasegawa. "Social modulation of contagious yawning in wolves." *PLoS One* 9, no. 8 (2014): e105963.

Walusinski, Olivier. "How yawning switches the default-mode network to the attentional network by activating the cerebrospinal fluid flow." *Clinical Anatomy* 27, no. 2 (2014): 201-209.

Giganti, F., and P. Salzarulo. "Yawning throughout life." In *The Mystery of Yawning in Physiology and Disease*, vol. 28, pp. 26-31. Karger Publishers, 2010.

Gallup, Andrew C., and Omar Tonsi Eldakar. "The thermoregulatory theory of yawning: what we know from over 5 years of research." *Frontiers in neuroscience* 6 (2013): 188.

Thompson, Simon BN. "Yawning, fatigue, and cortisol: expanding the Thompson Cortisol Hypothesis." *Medical hypotheses* 83, no. 4 (2014): 494-496.

Walusinski, Olivier. "Yawning: unsuspected avenue for a better understanding of arousal and interoception." *Medical hypotheses* 67, no. 1 (2006): 6-14.

[38] Wittgenstein, Ludwig. "Tractatus Logico-Philosophicus (trans. Pears and McGuinness)." (1961).

[39] Shakespeare, William. *Hamlet*. EP Dutton, 1905.

[40] Woolf, Virginia. "To the lighthouse." In *Collected Novels of Virginia Woolf*, pp. 177-334. Palgrave Macmillan, London, 1992.

[41] Flaubert, Gustave. *Madame bovary*. Bantam Classics, 1981.

[42] Miller, Richard E., and Ann Jurecic. *Habits of the creative mind*. Macmillan Higher Education, 2015.

[43] Winston Churchill Quotes. Goodread.com. 2020

https://www.goodreads.com/quotes/7738-from-now-on-ending-a-sentence-with-a-preposition-is, accessed July 11, 2020.

[44] Maggie, Stiefvater. "The Raven King." *NY: Scholastic* (2016).

[45] King, Stephen. *Rita Hayworth and Shawshank Redemption*. Scribner, 2020

[46] Place, Vanessa. *The Guilt Project: Rape, Morality, and Law*. Other Press, LLC, 2010.

[47] Place, Vanessa. "Rape jokes." *Studies in gender and sexuality*18, no. 4 (2017): 260-268.

[48] Vanessa Place, "Vanessa Place on Her Work with Rape Jokes," Artforum. April 2017.

[49] Shin, Ji-eun, Eunkook M. Suh, Kimin Eom, and Heejung S. Kim. "What does "happiness" prompt in your mind? Culture, word choice, and experienced happiness." Journal of Happiness Studies 19, no. 3 (2018): 649-662.

[50] Hammersley, Martyn, and Paul Atkinson. *Ethnography: Principles in Practice*. Routledge, 2007.

[51] Definition and examples of discourse. Thoughtco.com. 2020 https://www.thoughtco.com/discourse-language-term-1690464, accessed Dec 30, 2020.

[52] Harris, Zellig S. "Discourse analysis." In *Papers on syntax*, pp. 107-142. Springer, Dordrecht, 1981

[53] Fairclough, Norman. *Discourse and social change*. Vol. 10. Cambridge: Polity press, 1992.

[54] Marx, Karl. *The poverty of philosophy*. CH Kerr, 1920.

[55] Medgyes, Peter. *The non-native teacher*. London: Macmillan, 1994.

[56] Wilde, Oscar. *Intentions*. BoD-Books on Demand, 2018.

[57] Hoffer, Eric. *Between the devil and the dragon: The best essays and aphorisms of Eric Hoffer*. Harpercollins, 1982.

[58] Pagel, Mark. AZQuotes.com, Wind and Fly LTD, 2020. https://www.azquotes.com/quote/722970, accessed July 28, 2020.

[59] Newberg, Andrew, and Mark Robert Waldman. *Words can change your brain: 12 conversation strategies to build trust, resolve conflict, and increase intimacy*. Penguin, 2013.

[60] Waldman, Mark R, and Chris Manning. *NeuroWisdom: The new brain science of money, happiness and success*. Division, 2017

[61] Panksepp, Jaak, and Lucy Biven. *The archaeology of mind: neuroevolutionary origins of human emotions (Norton series on interpersonal neurobiology)*. WW Norton & Company, 2012.

[62] Interview with Cathy Price in *Fry's Planet Word*, a documentary series about language, written and presented by Stephen Fry.

[63] Adams, Douglas. *The hitch hiker's guide to the galaxy: a trilogy in five parts*. Random House, 1995.

[64] Im Shin, Hong, and Juyoung Kim. "Foreign language effect and psychological distance." *Journal of Psycholinguistic Research* 46, no. 6 (2017): 1339-1352.

[65] Mandela, Nelson. "If you talk to a man in a language he understands, that goes to his head. If you talk to him in his language, that goes to his heart." *Project Leadership* (2015): 215.

[66] Barrett, Lisa Feldman, and Eliza Bliss-Moreau. "Affect as a psychological primitive." *Advances in experimental social psychology* 41 (2009): 167-218.

Lindquist, Kristen A., Ajay B. Satpute, Tor D. Wager, Jochen Weber, and Lisa Feldman Barrett. "The brain basis of positive and negative affect: evidence from a meta-analysis of the human neuroimaging literature." *Cerebral cortex* 26, no. 5

(2016): 1910-1922.

[67] Eugenides, J., 2020. *Middlesex (Vol. 550)*. Anagrama.

[68] Widen, Sherri C. "Children's interpretation of facial expressions: The long path from valence-based to specific discrete categories." *Emotion Review* 5, no. 1 (2013): 72-77.

Widen, Sherri C., and James A. Russell. "Children's recognition of disgust in others." *Psychological Bulletin* 139, no. 2 (2013): 271.

[69] Lupyan, Gary, David H. Rakison, and James L. McClelland. "Language is not just for talking: Redundant labels facilitate learning of novel categories." *Psychological science* 18, no. 12 (2007): 1077-1083.

Barsalou, Lawrence W., Ava Santos, W. Kyle Simmons, and Christine D. Wilson. "Language and simulation in conceptual processing." *Symbols, embodiment, and meaning* (2008): 245-283.

Patterson, Karalyn, Peter J. Nestor, and Timothy T. Rogers. "Where do you know what you know? The representation of semantic knowledge in the human brain." *Nature reviews neuroscience* 8, no. 12 (2007): 976-987.

[70] Coup de Main interview with Mark Hoppus. Coupdemainmagazine.com. 2020. https://www.coupdemainmagazine.com/interviews/interview-mark-hoppus-blink-182s-new-album-california, accessed Nov 3, 2020

[71] Virgil, *Vergil's Eclogues* trans. Barbara Hughes Fowler, (Chapel Hill & London: The University of North Carolina Press, 1997), 30.

[72] 1 Cor. 13. accessed from https://biblehub.com/1_corinthians/

[73] King Jr, Martin Luther. "Loving your enemies." *The Papers of Martin Luther King, Jr* 4 (1957): 315-24.

[74] Helen Keller Quotes. BrainyQuote.com, BrainyMedia Inc, 2020.

https://www.brainyquote.com/quotes/helen_keller_143024, accessed July 28, 2020.

[75] Leo Buscaglia Quotes. BrainyQuote.com, BrainyMedia Inc, 2020. https://www.brainyquote.com/quotes/leo_buscaglia_142116, accessed July 28,

2020.

[76] Lao Tzu Quotes. BrainyQuote.com, BrainyMedia Inc, 2020. https://www.brainyquote.com/quotes/lao_tzu_387058, accessed July 28, 2020.

[77] Leu, Janxin, Jennifer Wang, and Kelly Koo. "Are positive emotions just as "positive" across cultures?." *Emotion* 11, no. 4 (2011): 994.

Russell, James A. "Culture and the categorization of emotions." *Psychological bulletin* 110, no. 3 (1991): 426.

Perlovsky, Leonid. "Language and emotions: emotional Sapir–Whorf hypothesis." *Neural Networks* 22, no. 5-6 (2009): 518-526.

Perlovsky, Leonid. "Language and emotions: emotional Sapir–Whorf hypothesis." *Neural Networks* 22, no. 5-6 (2009): 518-526.

[78] 10 of the best words in the world (that don't translate into English).Theguardian.com. 2020. https://www.theguardian.com/world/2018/jul/27/10-of-the-best-words-in-the-world-that-dont-translate-into-english, accessed July 28, 2020

[79] 10 of the best words in the world (that don't translate into English).Theguardian.com. 2020. https://www.theguardian.com/world/2018/jul/27/10-of-the-best-words-in-the-world-that-dont-translate-into-english, accessed July 28, 2020

[80] 10 of the best words in the world (that don't translate into English).Theguardian.com. 2020. https://www.theguardian.com/world/2018/jul/27/10-of-the-best-words-in-the-world-that-dont-translate-into-english, accessed July 28, 2020

[81] Translated by Irving Y. Lo; Chinese 春风得意马疾．一日看尽长安花(chun feng de yi ma ti ji, yi ri kan jin chang an hua)

[82] 10 of the best words in the world (that don't translate into English). Theguardian.com. 2020. https://www.theguardian.com/world/2018/jul/27/10-of-the-best-words-in-the-world-that-dont-translate-into-english, accessed July 28, 2020

[83] Jack, Rachael E., Oliver GB Garrod, Hui Yu, Roberto Caldara, and Philippe G. Schyns. "Facial expressions of emotion are not culturally universal." *Proceedings of the National Academy of Sciences* 109, no. 19 (2012): 7241-7244.

[84] Kircanski, Katharina, Matthew D. Lieberman, and Michelle G. Craske. "Feelings into words: contributions of language to exposure therapy." *Psychological science* 23, no. 10 (2012): 1086-1091.

[85] Lieberman, Matthew D., Naomi I. Eisenberger, Molly J. Crockett, Sabrina M. Tom, Jennifer H. Pfeifer, and B. M. Way. "Affect labeling disrupts amygdala activity in response to affective stimuli." *Psychological Science* 18, no. 5 (2007): 421-428.

[86] Tabibnia, Golnaz, Matthew D. Lieberman, and Michelle G. Craske. "The lasting effect of words on feelings: words may facilitate exposure effects to threatening images." *Emotion* 8, no. 3 (2008): 307.

[87] Payer, Doris E., Kate Baicy, Matthew D. Lieberman, and Edythe D. London. "Overlapping neural substrates between intentional and incidental down-regulation of negative emotions." *Emotion* 12, no. 2 (2012): 229.

[88] Panksepp, Jaak, and Lucy Biven. *The archaeology of mind: neuroevolutionary origins of human emotions (Norton series on interpersonal neurobiology).* WW Norton & Company, 2012

[89] Oosterwijk, Suzanne, Kristen A. Lindquist, Eric Anderson, Rebecca Dautoff, Yoshiya Moriguchi, and Lisa Feldman Barrett. "States of mind: Emotions, body feelings, and thoughts share distributed neural networks." *NeuroImage* 62, no. 3 (2012): 2110-2128.

Patterson, Karalyn, Peter J. Nestor, and Timothy T. Rogers. "Where do you know what you know? The representation of semantic knowledge in the human brain." *Nature reviews neuroscience* 8, no. 12 (2007): 976-987.

[90] Baumeister, Roy F., Ellen Bratslavsky, Catrin Finkenauer, and Kathleen D. Vohs. "Bad is stronger than good." *Review of general psychology* 5, no. 4 (2001): 323-370.

Sparks, Jehan, and Alison Ledgerwood. "Age attenuates the negativity bias in reframing effects." *Personality and Social Psychology Bulletin* 45, no. 7 (2019): 1042-1056.

[91] Emmons, Robert A. *Thanks!: How practicing gratitude can make you happier.* Houghton Mifflin Harcourt, 2008.

Wood, Alex M., Jeffrey J. Froh, and Adam WA Geraghty. "Gratitude and well-being: A review and theoretical integration." *Clinical psychology review* 30, no. 7 (2010): 890-905.

[92] For more information: Baer, Ruth A., and Jennifer Krietemeyer. "Overview of mindfulness-and acceptance-based treatment approaches." *Mindfulness-based treatment approaches: Clinician's guide to evidence base and applications* (2006): 3-27.

[93] For more information: Raffone, Antonino, Laura Marzetti, Cosimo Del Gratta, Mauro Gianni Perrucci, Gian Luca Romani, and Vittorio Pizzella. "Toward a brain theory of meditation." In *Progress in brain research*, vol. 244, pp. 207-232. Elsevier, 2019.

[94] David, Goleman. "Emotional intelligence." (1995).

[95] Wittgenstein, Ludwig. "Tractatus Logico-Philosophicus (trans. Pears and McGuinness)." (1961).

[96] Hazlitt, Henry. *Thinking as a Science.* Vol. 20. Createspace Independent Pub, 1916.

[97] Coe, Robert. "Improving education: A triumph of hope over experience." *Durham, United Kingdom: Durham University: Centre for Evaluation and Monitoring* (2013).

[98] Chomsky, Noam. "Language and problems of knowledge." *The Managua* (1988).

Chomsky, Noam. "On the nature, use and acquisition of language." *Language and meaning in cognitive science: cognitive issues and semantic theory* (1998): 1-20.

[99] Pinker, Steven. *The language instinct: How the mind creates language.* Penguin UK, 2003.

[100] Wolff, Phillip, and Kevin J. Holmes. "Linguistic relativity." *Wiley Interdisciplinary Reviews: Cognitive Science* 2, no. 3 (2011): 253-265.

[101] Casasanto, Daniel, Lera Boroditsky, Webb Phillips, Jesse Greene, Shima Goswami, Simon Bocanegra-Thiel, Ilia Santiago-Diaz, Olga Fotokopoulu, Ria Pita, and David Gil. "How deep are effects of language on thought? Time estimation in speakers of English, Indonesian, Greek, and Spanish." In *Proceedings of the Annual Meeting of the Cognitive Science Society*, vol. 26, no. 26. 2004.

[102] Vygotsky, Lev S. *Thought and language*. MIT press, 2012.

[103] Diaz, Rafael M., Laura E. Berk, and Rafael Diaz, eds. *Private speech: From social interaction to self-regulation*. Psychology Press, 2014.

[104] Perlovsky, Leonid, and Roman Ilin. "Brain. Conscious and unconscious mechanisms of cognition, emotions, and language." *Brain sciences* 2, no. 4 (2012): 790-834.

Schoeller, Félix, Leonid Perlovsky, and Dmitry Arseniev. "Physics of mind: experimental confirmations of theoretical predictions." *Physics of Life Reviews* 25 (2018): 45-68.

Perlovsky, Leonid. "Consciousness and free will, a scientific possibility due to advances in cognitive science." (2011).

Perlovsky, L. I. "Logic versus Mind." *Logica Universalis* (2012).

Perlovsky, Leonid, and Felix Schoeller. "Unconscious emotions of human learning." *Physics of life reviews* 31 (2019): 257-262.

[105] Kovács, Ágnes Melinda, and Jacques Mehler. "Flexible learning of multiple speech structures in bilingual infants." *science* 325, no. 5940 (2009): 611-612.

[106] Engel de Abreu, Pascale MJ, Anabela Cruz-Santos, Carlos J. Tourinho, Romain Martin, and Ellen Bialystok. "Bilingualism enriches the poor: Enhanced cognitive control in low-income minority children." *Psychological science* 23, no. 11 (2012): 1364-1371.

[107] Mercado, Joriene Gabriel. "Bilingual Brains." *The Cutting Edge: The Stanford Undergraduate Journal of Education Research* 2, no. 1 (2018).

Wang, Sam. (2011). "Bilingualism Will Supercharge Your Baby's Brain." Youtube

Bhattacharjee, Yudhijit. "Why bilinguals are smarter." *The New York Times* 17, no. 03 (2012).

[108] Bialystok, Ellen, Fergus IM Craik, and Morris Freedman. "Bilingualism as a protection against the onset of symptoms of dementia." *Neuropsychologia* 45, no. 2 (2007): 459-464.

Bialystok, Ellen, Fergus IM Craik, and Gigi Luk. "Bilingualism: consequences for mind and brain." *Trends in cognitive sciences* 16, no. 4 (2012): 240-250.

[109] Lövdén, Martin, Elisabeth Wenger, Johan Mårtensson, Ulman Lindenberger, and Lars Bäckman. "Structural brain plasticity in adult learning and development." *Neuroscience & Biobehavioral Reviews* 37, no. 9 (2013): 2296-2310.

Luo, Daiyi, Veronica PY Kwok, Qing Liu, Wenlong Li, Yang Yang, Ke Zhou, Min Xu, Jia-Hong Gao, and Li Hai Tan. "Microstructural plasticity in the bilingual brain." *Brain and Language* 196 (2019): 104654.

[110] Hart, Betty, and Todd R. Risley. *Meaningful differences in the everyday experience of young American children.* Paul H Brookes Publishing, 1995.

[111] Erard, Michael 2014 The New Work of Words. The Atlantic. Retrieved from https://www.theatlantic.com/technology/archive/2014/11/the-new-work-of-words/382277/.

Talbot, Margaret 2015 The Talking Cure. The New Yorker (January 12). Retrieved from https://www.newyorker.com/magazine/2015/01/12/talking-cure.

[112] Dehaene, Stanislas, Laurent Cohen, José Mcrais, and Régine Kolinsky. "Illiterate to literate: behavioural and cerebral changes induced by reading acquisition." *Nature Reviews Neuroscience* 16, no. 4 (2015): 234-244.

[113] Rueckl, Jay G., Pedro M. Paz-Alonso, Peter J. Molfese, Wen-Jui Kuo, Atira Bick, Stephen J. Frost, Roeland Hancock et al. "Universal brain signature of proficient reading: Evidence from four contrasting languages." *Proceedings of the National Academy of Sciences* 112, no. 50 (2015): 15510-15515.

[114] Hagelskamp, Carolin, Marc A. Brackett, Susan E. Rivers, and Peter Salovey. "Improving classroom quality with the RULER approach to social and emotional learning: Proximal and distal outcomes." *American Journal of Community*

Psychology 51, no. 3-4 (2013): 530-543.

[115] Building vocabulary is a powerful way to enhance your life and career. Jocrf.org. 2020. https://www.jocrf.org/resources/effective-ways-build-your-vocabulary, accessed September 2, 2020.

[116] You need a good vocabulary to succeed in business (and life). Vocabularyzoon.com. 2020 https://vocabularyzone.com/need-good-vocabulary-succeed-business-life/, accessed September 2, 2020.

[117] How to develop executive presence by improving your vocabulary. Vocabularyzoon.com. 2020 https://vocabularyzone.com/how-to-develop-executive-presence-by-improving-your-vocabulary/, accessed September 2, 2020.

[118] Aldous Huxley Quotes. BrainyQuote.com, BrainyMedia Inc, 2020. https://www.brainyquote.com/quotes/aldous_huxley_163031, accessed November 11, 2020.

[119] Maugham, W. Somerset. *The moon and sixpence*. Penguin, 2005.

[120] Text of J.K. Rowling's speech. News.harvard.edu. 2020 https://news.harvard.edu/gazette/story/2008/06/text-of-j-k-rowling-speech/. accessed July 11, 2020.

[121] Oliver, Mary. "The summer day." *New and selected poems* 1 (1992).

[122] Text of J.K. Rowling's speech. News.harvard.edu. 2020 https://news.harvard.edu/gazette/story/2008/06/text-of-j-k-rowling-speech/. accessed July 11, 2020.

[123] Interview with series creators Michelle and Robert King. BitterLawyer.com. 2020. http://bitterempire.com/the-good-wife-non-lawyers-behind-that-lawyer-show/, accessed Dec 2, 2020.

[124] Turner, Mark. *The literary mind: The origins of thought and language*. Oxford University Press, 1996.

[125] Bamberg, M., and I. H. Cooper. "Narrative analysis. APA handbook of research methods in psychology (Vol. 3)." (2011).

[126] Rose, Frank. *The art of immersion: How the digital generation is remaking Hollywood, Madison Avenue, and the way we tell stories.* WW Norton & Company, 2012.

[127] Polkinghorne, Donald E. *Narrative knowing and the human sciences.* Suny Press, 1988.

[128] Frankl, Viktor E. *Man's search for meaning.* Simon and Schuster, 1985.

[129] McAdams, Dan P. *The stories we live by: Personal myths and the making of the self.* Guilford Press, 1993.

[130] Rukeyser, Muriel. "The Speed of Darkness, 1968." *Collected Poems Of Muriel Rukeyser* (2005): 411-468.

[131] Altman, Alex. "Why the killing of George Floyd sparked an American uprising." *Time. June* 4 (2020).

[132] Miller, Liz Shannon (October 10, 2014). *IndieWire.* https://www.indiewire.com/2014/10/the-affair-creator-sarah-treem-on-constructing-the-rashomon-of-relationship-dramas-69194/, accessed September 2, 2020.

[133] Fitzgerald, F. Scott. *The great gatsby.* Broadview Press, 2007.

[134] Zadra, Antonio, Sophie Desjardins, and Eric Marcotte. "Evolutionary function of dreams: A test of the threat simulation theory in recurrent dreams." *Consciousness and Cognition* 15, no. 2 (2006): 450-463.

Gawain, Shakti. *Creative Visualization-: Use the Power of Your Imagination to Create What You Want in Your Life.* New World Library, 2016.

[135] 21 Ways to Make Your Vision Board More Powerful, Jack Canfield. https://www.jackcanfield.com/blog/how-to-create-an-empowering-vision-book/, accessed Nov 24, 2020.

[136] Panksepp, Jaak, and Lucy Biven. *The archaeology of mind: neuroevolutionary origins of human emotions (Norton series on interpersonal neurobiology).* WW Norton & Company, 2012.

www.ingramcontent.com/pod-product-compliance
Lightning Source LLC
Chambersburg PA
CBHW031300090426
42742CB00007B/537